DIARY OF A MUSLIM NOBODY

A collection of conscientiously compiled
commentary, societal reflections,
deeper introspections, parental poetry
and family frustrations...

Reaz Rahman

Grosvenor House
Publishing Limited

This book is published by
Grosvenor House Publishing Ltd
Link House
140 The Broadway, Tolworth, Surrey, KT6 7HT.
www.grosvenorhousepublishing.co.uk

A CIP record for this book
is available from the British Library

ISBN 978-1-83975-166-0

1ST Edition Print 2020.
Volume 5.

www.diaryofamuslimnobody.com
Insta: diaryofaMuslimNobody

Bi-smi llāhi r-raḥmāni r-raḥīm.

In the name of God, the Most Gracious, the Most Merciful.

For Imaani and Soraya

Acknowledgements

Special thanks to Nik, Liz, Lou, Zahra, Lucy, Kish, Debs, Rahima, Fatima, Sophia, Tanvir, Bubbly, Manish, Joelle, Mrs S. Kerry, Shaf & Zak.

Thank you to brothers Vaseem Mohammed and Raks for their wonderful contributions to the cover design.

Thank you to my amazing parents and Jasmine & Michael.

Contents

Preface

Diary of a Muslim Nobody attempts to reach out to society as a whole, regardless of affiliations and the social constructs of the labels we attach to ourselves, with the intention of reaching out to the commonality of the human experience.

Interweaving between personal reflections on the human experience and a commentary on global issues with touches of affection and humour through his relationship with his parents, Reaz attempts to demonstrate the multiplicity of experiences as we live our everyday lives.

"I have always been very aware of the power of language and the potential of its impact upon our own selves as individuals, our relationships and interactions and indeed our perceptions.

Perhaps the intrinsic relationship between our language and humankind may be best understood when we consider letters, by themselves, important in their own entity and when placed together becoming even more powerful as words — giving them substance and meaning.

In this instance, human beings may be aligned to letters — each important in our own right — and when we recognise our own value, we are then able to understand this in context to our relationship to one another.

In that moment, we are able to have the most profound and positive impact in our own lives and in the lives of others around us."

Introduction

It is a strange time indeed to be Muslim... In all honesty, speaking strictly for myself, I have never been more aware that this is the fundamental label that defines me. Perhaps, as we grow older, we become naturally more aware of what we want, and think about who we are as people and indeed who we want to be. Certainly, the world events over the last decade have compelled me to consider what my perspective is and what being a Muslim means to me. I never lived a life that was particularly 'Islamic' to be honest, and for a long time, I led a 'party life' filled with all the excesses associated with it, my only Muslim association being that I tried to always act in a kind way, without judging others, being a friend and doing my best to be a 'good person' (although not always achieving that) and therein I came to a realisation. Islam is not something that can be 'banned', it is not something to be defeated and neither does it seek to defeat. It is not something that seeks to terrorise others, and it is not something that requires apology. It is something intrinsic to human nature. Something that is part of one's soul. To love others, to live together, to seek justice, to have humility in one's perspectives and to negate arrogance, the

essence of peace. Such entities are natural to all human beings regardless of the labels we associate ourselves with if we each give ourselves the opportunity to think and question. Ignorance is bred just as knowledge is acquired, so the only question then becomes — how aware each of us is that essentially our differences are none...

The phrase a 'Muslim Nobody' is not to demean or indeed be detrimental in perceived self-worth, as is often mistakenly assumed. More accurately, it is to acknowledge that everybody is somebody and more so, that in the moments where we interact with one another we are not just somebody, we are everything, if we follow the decree of the Creator and live in gratitude of what is the now of the present moment gifted to us...

In acknowledgement of Him, we are each the universe and all that it contains, the vastness of His glory and greatness permeating our thoughts and feelings and allowing us to grow both through our individual acknowledgement and our interdependent state...

Without Him, limited by our self-driven arrogance to definitively define...

With Him, to be at peace with our humility, in that all glory and knowledge is with Him and surely, He guides us to the very best of answers...

Our equality, our oneness, our obligation to elevate each and every one to His highest ranks through kindness, love and compassion... encompassing all that acknowledge Him with the exception of none.

* As I write this book the world is witnessing the advent the 'Corona Crisis', a phenomenon that has literally taken over global society, compelling us to re-examine the way we have been living up to this point and inevitably causing us to question how we will live in the future. As we are all living in a literal 'lockdown', perhaps the truth of really understanding and valuing something only once it has gone has never been more deeply understood...

Rather than being avoided and ignored, our connection to our elders and their safety should, given the chance, be embraced and cherished, whilst we are able to hold them close.

Equally important as having time for ourselves, is to acknowledge and understand the significance of our interdependence and our collective commonalities and identity.

Our social distancing now crucially helps us to appreciate the value of the intimacy and miraculous status of every human interaction.

Our responsibility to the most vulnerable in society — essentially understanding our very own vulnerability — is no different, regardless of race, religion, class or any other societal structures.

In addition to the crisis of Corona the world, humanity is facing an uprising against the poison of systemic racism against our black brothers and sisters in humanity.

Across many cities and regions of the world, human beings from all denominations are physically protesting against the inequalities that continue to contaminate black lives in a message of resistance and need to recognise the need for equality and justice that has been stripped away from black people by institutional and societal structures which create and perpetuate the message their lives are less worthy.

Genetically/Scientifically/Biologically we are all 99.9% recurring the same, if we are simply to go by the facts. Every other perceived difference, is nothing more than a social construct & in some instances such as 'race relations', nothing more than indicative of humankind's arrogance & hatred of themselves.

Of course racism & prejudice exists in amongst and between cultures. Denial of this reality will only further exacerbate a problematic issue that is prevalent poison in all comm-unities.

The disparity of what we deem to be our lived realities, based on the colour of our skin, is a detriment to every single one of us & it is simply not enough to deny or shy away simply because it does not suite what we want to be true.

We are all rightly accountable for our actions.

Every time a human beings life is taken, every time they are treated differently, every time their hope is lost, every time their voice is intentionally unheard or muted, every time there is inequity in our inter-actions, based on their race, the colour of their skin, in every instance we don't speak up, then a part of our integrity dies.

It is about facing our collective truths for all that they are, for only then will we begin the journey to our solutions. Denial of the different & unequal experiences will only lead to further suffocation of possible solutions.

We can each only begin with acknowledging our own reality and realise there are no 'others', more so, only us, living together, albeit some-times very differently, together, as one huma-nity.

We all have an equal right to call this Earth our home, to find in it a place of safety and to be afforded the human rights of respect, acknowledgement and dignity in every conceiv-able capacity of existence. Should we be blessed enough to live through the challenges we face, we should be enabled to live in a cleaner, more considered way, so that we can all feel less suffocated by our own arrogance and destructive consumption and be able to really live, as we all should and breathe...

Insha'Allah.

Family Frustrations and Societal Reflections

The 'Greatness' of Great Britain was made so, standing not on the shoulders of giants but on the blood spilt of everyday people in their millions. The masses of both the indigenous British working classes and those inhabitants of foreign lands — lands pillaged and raped of their natural resources. 'The Empire' did not bring civilisation to the lands it conquered, rather, in many instances, it destroyed civilisations and cultures that had existed through the ages and thereby distorted historical facts.

As our armed forces continue to be sent to foreign lands for reasons we don't understand, as they are sent out to the sea to turn away people we label 'refugees' who are simply looking for safety, perhaps we would do well to remember, the greatness of any country lies not in conquest, dominance and control, but, more accurately, in recognising that everyone deserves to live and be free.

Amongst my very earliest memories in life is Mum grafting for what seemed like forever at the sewing machine and my dad, although super loving when there, leaving to work so early in the morning it was still dark and coming back from work only when it was dark again. For a very long time, that was what I knew as the norm. Despite working the age-old cliché of 'all the hours under the sun', I remember one constant was them taking it in turns to teach me the alphabet and, later, words from the dictionary. When I really come down to the root cause of what has led me to write, this is undoubtedly the original source.

My parents' story is one that was repeated a thousand times by Bangladeshi and Asian minority families throughout the 60s and 70s, arriving from the Indian subcontinent with a legacy of the remnants of Empire, in the foreign land of all lands, the land of the Queen herself. Literally arriving with nothing in their hand, to a place with an alien culture and alien language, with very little with which to build their destiny, other than one another, their faith and their resilience. Trying to make it when they were openly not even deemed eligible for public housing based on their ethnicity and the resulting social status, sharing and squatting a room with five other families in buildings deemed not fit for purpose for the indigenous white community, whilst working multiple menial jobs, literally to save pennies for themselves and for the family members they had left behind, who were relying on their successful status as

'Londonis'. You know, in all the years I saw my dad working, right up until when he retired, I don't think I ever saw him not take his lunch to work — either egg sandwiches or peanut butter and jam — a bit like Paddington Bear; in a funny way they had more in common than just their sandwiches. (Regrettably, I used to have to take the egg sandwiches on the times I got to go on school trips — hardboiled egg sandwiches and the smell of the coach will never be a good combination, and I doubt there will ever be destination worthy of enduring the combined smell and the resulting feeling they induce)... Anyways I remember I asked Dad once why it was he didn't just buy lunch when he was out... to which his response quite simply was how could he ever waste £2 on lunch when he could save that money and send it 'back home' and that would be enough to feed a whole family?

My parents taught me of the freedom struggle of the Palestinians and Muhammed Ali and Mandela, and of their own identity struggle, having themselves been part of the very first generation that could call themselves Bangladeshi against a backdrop of the sacrifices of the lives of millions of their peers, family members and elders, in what has been widely accepted as amongst the bloodiest of movements for freedom and independence in modern times. Identity? Imagine. Referred to as 'Pakis' in the country where you lived, originating from a place where you were fighting for the acceptance of your Bangladeshi identity with Pakistan itself, contending

7

with internal prejudice within the Asian and Bangladeshi community, struggling together as minority Asians against the racism you all collectively suffered, identifying beyond politics with both your fellow Muslims and by way of economics, your fellow working-class neighbours, regardless of whatever other social labelling you all happened to fall into...

Education starts and finishes really at whatever one calls one's home, whatever dynamic that may take. One parent, two parents, no parents; our earliest experiences are what fundamentally shape us and our character and how we perceive the world which we are in for better or worse... Honestly, throughout all of their struggles and the resilience they equipped themselves with, I can't ever really remember my parents speak against anything other than injustice and, even then, never ever speaking of hating those that had inflicted or caused the societal or personal injustice, rather, focusing on the need to make the right choice as a Muslim.

I write this book as a collection of personal reflections and reflective commentaries, as someone who is unqualified by any scholarly measure from either an academic or religious perspective. I am far from well-read by any standards and at best, can sometimes string a sentence together that others can relate to... and therein, perhaps, is the very point of this book.

Beyond the social constructs of identity that we place on ourselves and that are placed upon us, we are all intrinsically related through our commonality as human beings. My diary is the diary of every person that reads my writing, in that our understanding of what we know to be human will be drawn essentially that much closer together and therein is a possible path to our collective, universal peace...

Word

Our choice of words in how we treat one another and express ourselves is, without doubt, one of the most powerful choices we have. Our words, if we so choose, are a gateway to our innermost thoughts, without which, our understanding of one another would otherwise be extremely limited. They articulate not only our perceptions but are also an indication of our inner character. While through our choices of words, we can mock and belittle one another, through words we can collectively lift one another up and inspire each other, provide comfort and security, give hope and express love. To endure to find the right words so that we may keep positively moving forward together, irrespective of the negative words that may sometimes be used against us, is a precious autonomy that we must always value.

Parental Poetry 1

Mum:

'Mila Milee — Tik Takh.' As with most phrases
in different languages, my attempt to provide
an exact meaning into English would most
probably result in a certain degree of 'lost
in translation'.

As I grew up, my understanding of this
essential bit of advice from Mum kind of
meant 'mix with others with kindness and
consideration and therein is a path to your
personal peace'. Many years later, I am more
aware of the physical, emotional and psychological barriers people place between one
another, which in turn results in mass
isolation from human interaction and our
consequential understanding of each other,
and I realise what a profound statement of
love Mum's simple sentence of advice really
was.

Notes

Dad:

When I was really young, Dad used to tell me for every grain of rice wasted, I would have to ask God for forgiveness 100,000 times. I wasn't exactly sure how much that was, other than that it was really a lot as there were lots of grains on my plate, and rather than trying to work it out, it was easier to simply finish all the rice. Throughout my life, the message my dad had given me became a part of my subconscious and up until this very moment has shaped my perspectives on life: To value even the very smallest of things, to appreciate everything we have been blessed with, to think about others with less and to appreciate the Provider of our sustenance. My dad. A supposedly 'uneducated' man, educating his son the most valuable of life lessons through simply a grain of rice... The words we use with one another can have the most profound effects, such effects may only be truly appreciated and understood years later. The legacy of our words and interactions transcends generations, and through pure love and intentions, our blessings educate and inspire.

Notes

The people who bring energy to us, who encourage and invigorate us, who support and solidify us, whose spirit permeates all those around them, challenging the perceptions of what we believe to be possible, who complement and complete us. The everyday, extraordinary people each of us to one another...

Notes

Family Frustrations:
Morning

Dad: Son, fill this form out and give it back asap.

Me: OK, no problem, Dad. What is it?

Dad: What's with the questions? Do as your dad says, but if you must know, it's an opinion poll questionnaire.

Me: I was just asking...

Dad: Well, less talking and more doing would result in you knowing what it was, wouldn't it?

Me: Dad, don't you think you should fill it out since it's about your opinions?

Dad: Yes, I do think I should fill it out. That's why I've told you to do it?

Me: No, I mean, as in *you* fill out the form yourself?

Dad: Listen, son, I didn't send YOU to get an education for ME not to have an opinion, now hurry up and get writing... honestly sometimes you get very lazy...

Me: But what if you and I have differing opinions?

Dad: What?

Me: Nothing... I'll get it sorted...

Dad: Yo, son, remember I told you I need those passport photos of you to sort out that account in Bangladesh?

Me: Yeah, Dad, I told you I'm waiting as I haven't been looking that great this week.

Dad: Waiting? Waiting for what? Because if you're waiting to look as good as me, you'll have a long wait as that's never gonna happen.

Me: Right. Dad, I'm just waiting as I've been looking a bit rough and the picture's permanent once done.

Dad: Don't worry about looking rough, you've always looked like that, no point in worrying about it now.

Me: OK, thanks, Dad.

Dad: Good now we've got that cleared up, get that sorted today, yeah?

Mum: When you answer your mobile, you shouldn't hold it next to your head.

Dad: Now what are you going on about?

Mum: What I'm going on about, as usual, is good advice, as it can give you brain damage.

Dad: Here we go 'the Doctor' is here again.

Mum: Doctor or not, keeping the phone next to your head can affect your brain.

Dad: Well, you never answer any of your calls, so that makes you safe then!

Mum: I don't need to answer your call as I know you will just talk rubbish like now.

Dad: Well for the rest of us who actually answer their phone we need to put it next to our head as that's where our ears are and we do this thing called listening — you might not know what that is as it has never been your strong point...

Mum: Actually, you know what — don't worry about the phone next to your brain, actually, as there isn't really that much to damage!

Dad: Here he comes, mad-boy with his 100 trainers and not one wife.

Me: Salaam, Dad.

Dad: What's that? Yet another pair of new trainers, son? How many is that, 1,001?

Me: They're not that new, I just don't wear them that much.

Dad: Son, I've told you many times. Don't try and outsmart me.

Me: They are limited edition and nice for the summer.

Dad: Limited edition for the summer? That just means there's not as many people as mad as you to sell them to, boy.

Me: OK, thanks, Dad.

Corona Conversations:

Me: (Coming down the stairs) Oh good, you're clapping for the NHS, well done!

Mum: I thought there was going to be an ambulance driving past so they could know how proud we are.

Me: No, Mum, I think the ambulances would be slightly busy at this time.

Mum: Well, how will they hear us then?

Me: I'm sure they will know.

Mum: How? There are no doctors living near us — of course, I did tell you to study harder at school then you could've been the local doctor and heard everyone and told your doctor friends.

Me: Yeah, OK, Mum. You concentrate on clapping.

Dad: Maybe if you were a doctor you would've got a wife by now...

Allahsakes.

Corona Conversations:

Mum: Shall we do NHS clapping before we pray?

Me: Well, by the time you finish praying, the clapping will be done.

Mum: OK, I'm sure Allah won't mind.

Dad: I'm the best at clapping; leave it to me — son, you look really thirsty after fasting all day.

Me: So, you're tryna say you want a cup of tea, Dad, then?

Dad: Yes, if you insist, son.

Me: 'Please' you mean.

Dad: Well, you don't need to say please, I've said yes, go ahead already. It's like permission.

Me: No, I mean you forgot to say please? You always do this... Why don't you ever just ask for the tea?

Dad: Should a man need to ask his son for tea? I can't believe you just said that — it's OK, I understand, you're tired from fasting, no need for sorry... now let me clap, you go...

Dad: Oi, what was that job you do, boy? I've got a family with a daughter asking about you.

Me: Dad, do we have to go through this again?

Dad: Well, apparently, we do since you refuse to sort yourself out.

Me: Well, it's not going to work out, but I'm a behavioural mentor.

Dad: What mental?

Me: No MenTOR.

Dad: What kind of job calls itself mental? Couldn't you get a normal job with a normal name? Why not be a teacher?

Me: I don't want to be a teacher.

Dad: Well, I'll tell them you're a teacher, let's just keep it simple.

Me: Well, why can't you just say what I do?

Dad: Listen, who wants someone to drive them mental? Saying you're mental can wait — they'll find out soon enough after a few conversations. Teacher — that's what we'll say you do. The same thing. Everyone wants someone that can teach them...

Me: Well it's kind of the same but different...

Dad: You see. That's always been your problem — you're kind of the same but different...

Ramadan Conversations:

Me: Would you like some tea? Although we may not have enough time before fasting is meant to start...

Dad: So, you making it or what?

Me: I'm just saying I can make it, just the time factor to be aware of.

Dad: Less saying more doing that's the problem with your generation, boy, I've told you this already.

Me: I am doing. Me making you aware has no bearing on the kettle boiling time whilst I'm saying it.

Dad: You trying to be clever again, son, I've told you this too — it doesn't suit you so don't try.

Mum: He's just making you aware.

Dad: Making me aware? You don't offer someone tea and then pressure them before you've even made it — so I'm making him aware. How's someone even meant to fast without having a cup of tea anyway?

Me: It's ready now.

Dad: See, boy, that wasn't that hard was it? As if Allah wouldn't want to give us enough time to have tea — don't start saying that in

public, this is what gives Muslims a bad rep... You having yours black, are you?

Me: Yes, as I don't have dairy milk, we've spoken about this, many times.

Dad: Why don't you just give it a rest, son? Well, at least you're not putting that nut juice in this time.

Me: It's called almond milk.

Dad: Well, whatever, it's not normal is it?

Me: Actually, lots of people have it now.

Dad: Yeah, OK. Don't go telling girls you have that stuff; it's taking you long enough to get a wife as it is.

Me: What's that got to do with it?

Dad: Well, if I have to explain that to you, son, then no wonder you ain't married... anyways it's Ramadan let's not go into all that right now...

Ramadan Conversations:

Me: Was that someone at the door earlier?

Dad: Yes, a woman asking for money.

Me: It could've been an angel in disguise sent from Allah to test you.

Dad: Well it wasn't.

Me: How do you know? Allah sometimes sends them in human form...

Dad: Well, she comes every year at Ramadan.

Me: That could mean something!

Dad: Yes, it means she is targeting us. Besides, what kind of angel asks for more money once you have given them some?

Me: Well, Allah could be putting a further test on you to see the extent of your generosity!

Dad: Listen, boy, next time, I tell you what — you get tested as it seems to me everyone else passed the test of ignoring the doorbell and leaving it to me!

Deeper Introspections 1

'What will people say?' Probably one of the most frustrating phrases a young Muslim person hears growing up. However, within this question is arguably amongst the best examples of selfless wisdom we can each aspire to, that maybe gets lost in parental translation. Western society is fundamentally individualist in both perception and interpretation, wherein the focus is on the self and how one progresses and evolves to benefit our own life. Comparatively, Islamic 'eastern' societies on multifaceted levels, traditionally promote the ideal of our interdependence and indeed inter-reliance between one another through generations. The focus in such instances is not on the individual and their own personal happiness, rather the focus is on seeking one's individual happiness in the context of our place in wider society. Perhaps, rather than asking 'what would people say?' the question is more accurately 'how will your actions impact upon and affect others?' and indeed, if we were to all ask ourselves such questions, rather than being frustrated, our own lives would be much more considered, both to ourselves and the world in which we live...

Notes

Such are the multitude of our personal wrongs in every one of us, that if truly they were exposed, none would be able to face each other, for fear of embarrassment and shame. All glory to He, that knows each and every one of those wrongs, yet protects and shields us, each from one another, with His love and protection, gracing us with His infinite blessings of grace and opportunities to live in humility and beyond the arrogance with which we often perceive the mistakes of others.

Notes

In this journey of life, we find we are inextricably interlinked to people through our emotions and experiences. While relationships between our friends and families are overtly apparent, we often are not aware of the souls we touch and reach out to. Our words, our actions, our thoughts, our energy, our very example just by living life, each through our own nuanced and unique interpretation, can provide the most positive perspectives, sometimes in instances where darkness has long resided. It is possible for each of us to be a light to each other, guiding the paths of where we each step and ensuring we walk on beautiful travels... such is the beauty of human interaction and the miracle of life.

Notes

Perhaps the truest sign of the purest of love between people, is that through their common unity, each one feels individually more free.

Notes

The way in which we each interconnect with one another is perhaps one of the greatest evidences of our Creator. Our inability to articulate such connections, even amongst the most eloquent of speakers is indeed one of our most precious of signs, often transcending our conscious perceptions, understood only through our subconscious understanding. Knowing within our heart and the depths of our soul, we are blessed to have the presence of others in our life is a sign within itself of our Creator and indicative of His love, which reaches beyond our ability to comprehend, through mere rationed intelligence and is central to understanding our own humanity and the essence of faith itself.

Notes

If we measure our success and personal wealth simply on the basis of our financial and monetary status, then, as human beings, we are hugely undervaluing ourselves.

Notes

Every so often we are fortunate enough to be paying attention as we look up into the beauty of the night sky, we see one star that gleams brighter and more beautiful, much in the same way as those special people we are blessed to come across every so often, their enigmatic aura beyond any attributable accurate description, their unexpected presence in our lives, surely the most blessed of gifts...

Notes

Perhaps accepting the condition of our own human fragility is so intrinsic to our own unique being, that embracing those very sensitivities are essential to the very strengths we each need to grow...

Notes

It is not that the world does not need more successful people, for surely, it does. More accurately, the world, made up of each one us, needs to recognise success is not defined through monetary riches or misconstrued notions of social standing. Success, both individually and collectively, is defined through our connections, reaching out and looking within, through love, humility, respect, dignifying, honouring and elevating both ourselves and all those we live through, in this experience we recognise as life.

Notes

Human interactions are the most curious of entities. Even in knowing one another, what we know for 'a fact' really is nothing at all. Even the most intimate of connections and the best of intentions are on the presumption of understanding and an appreciation with time and experience assisting our understanding and our basis of knowledge. Reciprocation of our actions is neither assured, or definitive. The extent to which the possibility to affect one another through our actions and words is mysterious, magical and miraculous and therein is the beauty of what our relationships mean. The possibility of new perspectives and the permission to enter the most sacred of precious places — the very heart and soul of another being is a privilege of the highest honour indeed. 'Surely there are signs for those who reflect'...

Notes

There are people in life that despite appearing to be showered with an abundance of good fortune and blessings will still be envious of others, viewing any gain others achieve with arrogance and contempt.

Conversely, (in apparent comparison), there are those with seemingly very little themselves, who love and support the good they witness happening to others and genuinely feel happiness for and to them.

Perhaps this example is one of the most profound examples of outward deceptions and inner reality perceptions.

Those of real wealth, are those whose light of love guides their path as they travel in their journeys of life, the good they see in and for others, serving as both inspiration and encouragement to themselves.

The person of envy and jealousy has a perception obscured with hate, the darkness within themselves never allowing them to feel real care and happiness for others and subsequently a shadow clouds even their appreciation of their very own blessings.

Each of us has a choice in life — 'a lover or a hater' essentially, let us each strive for the real riches of life, showing love in abundance and allowing it to guide our inner thoughts and outer journey, creating a world of wealth for us all.

Notes

As a person, I have a multitude of hypocrisies, struggling with myself and what actually is my wealth? My thoughts and actions and my (lack of) satisfaction, the disparities between my outward identity and the inner reality, my goals and desired destinations, the actuality of my life situations, the version of me that is the sinner, to be very honest, is often the winner... What version of me is real from what I choose to reveal? And for all these instances that occur every day, in a multitude of moments in every conceivable way, I am eternally grateful for the blessed month of Ramadan. A month where I can't eat in the light of the sun, having to wait until night has begun, moreover I am given the chance to feed my soul — a gift from my Creator to make me more whole...

Notes

It is written that as one places their forehead to the ground in prayer to the Creator of all that is both seen and unseen, our personal sins and wrongs fall from our shoulders by decree of His love and mercy. As I grow older and more aware of my faults and wrongdoing, so the sense of inner peace that overcomes me in this position of 'sujood' is like no other, wishing sometimes my head could stay connected to His earth forever, as even if I was to stay there from now to infinity, His protection and love is always never-ending...

Notes

The qualities of our Creator are fascinating to ponder and reflect upon, an omnipotent entity beyond that which even the most scholarly amongst us is able to comprehend and before which, all, without exception, are humbled. The Creator, who provides and sustains with such glorified beauty and blessings knowing that we will be 'OK', simply is not enough. The Creator whose countless examples of exact equations of creation are so precise, to attribute mere luck or chance to such instances, simply make no sense... The Creator who promises each and every one of us justice, of our existence and all that happens both in our considered consciousness and that which is far beyond... The Creator who decrees us to love, wherein even the most knowledgeable of us knows not what will happen, ordaining to believe and seek comfort and live, knowing we are blessed from above...

Social Commentary 1

Words

'You're all right'
They used to tell me
'It's the others we don't like'
Apparently, there were different types of
  'Paki'
Apparently, some deserved a fright
Normally the ones that had just arrived
Were the biggest victims of hate
Even some of my own called them 'freshies'
Wasn't this just racist in a different way?
Judged and belittled by those whose approval
  they seek
Looked down upon and seen as weak
And the irony is I wasn't so different, many
  years before
They seemed to have forgotten their hate now
- to me, those memories are still raw
To such a degree they defined me
And how I live today
Looking at how language affects us and always
  searching for a better way
For just as words can scare us, they can also
  teach us love
And just to know things could be different,
  how could we ever use them enough?

Notes

The total amount of estimated wealth made from the Empire across the world is certainly in its billions, if not trillions in a financial context. The multiples of lives changed forever, even up to modern-day contemporary society, immeasurable.

Notes

Commonwealth

Just a fancy word for colony
Symbolic, of how you hold the monopoly
There's no wealth in labelling me minority
Threaten my right to exist, then offer an
  apology
A history of pillaging foreign lands
Raped and enslaved, by your thieving hands
And now we're meant to appreciate
How you made us civilised
Indoctrination, education, systematic set of
  lies
A constant message set agenda of the right
  to police me
Let me know you control the right to my
  liberty
Suppress my voice and take away my rights to
  be heard
Propaganda to the point where we can't see
  the true word
Your deadly domination doesn't make you
  better than me
You see I simply believe everyone should be
  free
I reject your notion of modern liberal
  democracy
I reject the image and the fallacy
I believe in true freedom for every person
  on earth
I believe everyone is of equal worth
Come correct, if you're coming at all
Break down every brick of your divisory wall
Smash your glass ceiling set to contain me
Only after all this is done will my people
  ever be free

Notes

If only the wealth was really as common as
    described
And not just propaganda and more accurately
    lies
A legacy of all that you stole
To take your status so high, whilst keeping
    us so low
And now you dare to say you will 'repatriate'
Those people who contributed to make you so
    great?
Report, deport without a second thought
Families once again torn apart and left
    distraught
Apparently, the label of 'foreign national'
Gives you the green light to act so cruel
To uproot those who call this land home
Dividing families and leaving people alone
Apparently to you, their purpose is served
Is removing their right to this land really
    what they deserve?
Your deeper message to us all is clearly
    heard
Minority ethnic belonging here? — An idea
    absurd.
Talk of equality in days past
Replaced with the message that we will
    always be second class
Was it really all of us that were really so
    weak?
That made you so dominant and resulted in
    our defeat?
Or was it that our agenda was different
Seeking to create a better life — not of your
    hate belligerent
As looked upon us all as worth less then you

Notes

Just because of our beliefs and cultures and
    different hues
And when eventually nothing is left but
    white
Will that then, to you, be a pure and
    wonderful sight?
Of course, you will allow those of us who can
    'contribute'
Those who work hard and add to your loot
Divide the masses as if we are not all one
Ruling elite game strategy since the day it
    began.
Windrush warriors sent to Jamaica
Do you really think less immigrants makes
    Britain any greater?

Notes

'Immigrant' contributions to the UK economy are estimated to exceed £25 billion annually. While progress continues to be made in many areas of life, despite this fiscal fact, racism and prejudice based on fear of 'the other,' remain a part of the accepted experiences of the lives of the many immigrants that call Great Britain home.

Notes

Great Hate Nation

Why is it that you hate me?
Is it because of all the things you've taken?
Claimed as your own for our Great Nation?
What exactly is it?
Were my people only meant to visit?
Leave, once the dirty work was done?
And it seems yet another new chapter of hate
  has begun
Over and over in your history
A cycle repeated perpetually
Oh, so Great Nation of bigotry
Why, why is it that you hate me so?
I would really and truly like to know
What is it that you fear?
Simply, that I don't sit with you over a
  beer?
But you love our food and all the rest,
  right?
Don't you recall how your ships and soldiers
  came by night?
Entered into all those territories
We would've welcomed you as friends had you
  not seen us as enemies
Taking and raping all that you could
Not seeing your wrong, more so believing you
  should
Justified through your entitled mentality
That you were always so much better than me
And now you tell me I should be grateful
If I speak up for my rights, you tell me I'm
  hateful
But it is you in reality filled with hate
Failing to see what really makes this nation
  so great

Notes

Refusing to embrace our difference and
  diversity
Rejecting any notion, we're equal
  universally
And the irony it would appear of all the
  great nations
Who have terrifying racism within their
  creation and foundation
Have turned the narrative to such a degree
We are supposedly the terrorist enemy
No regards for our contributions
Brought our parents here on lies and
  delusions
That we are a welcome and valued entity
Reality — the accepted enemy implicitly
So, why is it that you hate me?
If we both sat together, could you really
  tell me freely?
Or could you not even do that because of your
  hate?
Is that the very thing that makes your
  nations great?
The thing is if you hate me and I hate you
  back
If we each hate each other for fear of attack
Then how will either of us ever really grow?
Until we put hate aside how we ever gonna
  know?
'Stop the immigration to this Great Nation!'
'Stop the inflation, downsize the
  population!'
No thought of the contribution, facts in
  dilution
No thought of the diversity, only talk of
  adversity
Question. How did you even come to be?

Notes

What do you really know about me?
Your only contact with me after the pub for a
  curry?
Commodified minority, labelled unskilled
All the while it was us you used to make
  society build
Identity mystery, reassigned history
If you really knew all that came from us
Doubt you would really see yourself as so
  much above
And if you were to take away all that we gave
Or more accurately what you stole as you
  rode in on your 'Rule Britannia' wave
As you stared back at your own reflection
Thinking of all you turned away and rejected
  for your own protection
You would realise how you were left with
  nothing at all
And know yourself how the supposed mighty
  fall
You would break down your xenophobic
  barriers and racist walls
You would welcome us all in with humility
Knowing I need you and you need me.

Notes

The British Raj is estimated to have taken over $45 trillion from the Indian subcontinent, a lasting legacy of Colonialism, tearing apart the land and its people on her departure, employing the tried and tested strategy of divide and conquer for years to follow...

Notes

Raj's Wreckage

And maybe 1947 was the exact date
That started the message of internal hate
Again and again, strategy of conquer and
 divide
Independence? One big Lie
While hate exists, we simply exist in defeat
How Mountbatten would laugh at such a
 treacherous treat!
Should've known back then the Empire Strikes
 Back
Not to defend itself, more malicious attack
To destroy the truth of how we all lived
 together
Only leaving our land once united, divided
 forever
The truth of any rulers is their legacy
Turning those that lived together, into
 everyday enemies
Classifying to cause division
Manipulation of different faith and religion
Now one to be made into a second-class
 citizen?
Yet another story of minority oppression
Will humanity ever learn its own lessons?
The masses so entrenched in indoctrination
They got us believing being 'fair and
 lovely' is our salvation
And whether Masjid, Mandir or Gurdwara
Isn't the core of the message to live as
 equals together?
Evidence of shared history the Mahal of Taj
Proof if needed we lived before the Raj

Notes

Back then weren't we all living together in
   Hindustan?
Managed to live through our problems all as
   one?
And now the politically corrupt set a rule
   of identity
Mass protest by all those that want to live
   freely
Standing together in love and solidarity
Rejection of the hate of the government of
   Modi
Allegedly more camps of concentration
For the victim faith persuasion
Replication of Hitler's history
Remember he didn't get no victory!
Yet another story of the terrified called the
   terroriser
The truth becoming apparent to all who see
   where the lies are
As we watch city upon city fall apart and
   burn
Lives destroyed with nowhere to turn
Becomes harder every day to say 'not my
   concern'
Mainstream media causing confusion
A distorted agenda to add to the illusion
No unbiased source we are able to trust
To act for the innocent is a must
The everyday people whose lives are taken
Collateral damage their value forsaken
Supposedly divided religiously
Taking away from the fact of one community
Agendas of the powerful to divide and
   destroy
Read upon history — it's an age-old ploy

Notes

Which belief permits you to take the life of
    another?
Are we not all taught to show love for our
    neighbour?
The legacy of self-destruction will long
    reside
Far beyond those victims who at hate's hands
    died
Are we not all meant to live in one
    community?
I no better then you — you no better than me?
Are we not meant to live in one community?
In peace, together in unity?
Why don't we acknowledge how people have
    lived together peacefully?
Does it really matter who's doing the
    killing?
As long as we each let it happen, ain't we
    all sinning...?
And the Pied Piper of fascism visited an
    ancient land
With his Trumped-up agenda and political
    under hand
Reinforce a rhetoric of hate
Planned incitement and his news so fake
Leaving a legacy of destruction
Murderer Modi under his instruction
The police were meant to protect me
Instead they looked away indifferently
As the gangs of the government came to my
    community
And raped away my dignity
Despite our disputes we always lived
    together
How will we now ensure the damage done
    doesn't last for forever?

Notes

They betrayed their ancient belief
Such deceit rarely seen
To think it was my religion that was meant to
  be extreme
My neighbourhood chastised
Based on fascist lies
I thought 'they' weren't to harm a living
  thing
Seeing God in everything?
Yet they saw no part of Him in me
No regard for my honour and chastity
Forever my memory now scarred
A target for hate just because of who you are
No right to live because of my belief
Mocked 'where was my God to bring me relief?'
Forgetting He was the same as yours
And that you had broken His most sacred laws
Taking the lives of the other
Causing another to suffer
Know that people of all faiths tried to
  protect
True people who questioned how they could
  possibly neglect
What they could see and the pain in my eyes
They chose to look past the fascist lies
Recognised our common bonds and land
Reached out with their helping hands
Maybe that wasn't so commonly reported in
  the news
With their political agenda aimed to confuse
And when the hurricane of hate settles down
Maybe then you'll ask how did you allow
My people and family not to live
And how will you then of yourselves forgive?

Notes

Bordering between India and Pakistan: it is estimated since 'independence' over 70,000 innocent people have lost their lives in this disputed territory.

Notes

Kashmiri Vibes

Kashmiri vibes
For Kashmiri tribes
Kashmiri vibes
Tryna just stay alive
Freedom Cries
From being occupied
Media blackout to hide the crimes
We don't want no genocide
Kashmiri vibes
From Kashmiri lives
Independent people of pride
More than just a political prize
For independence will uprise
Kashmiri vibes
For Kashmiri tribes
Let's live in peace and put war aside
No winners when nations collide
No winners when armies strike
No winners when people live in fright
Peace is the only side
Peace is over what we should preside
Peace shouldn't be denied
To Kashmiri vibes
Just tryna stay alive

Notes

It is estimated around 1% of the population
of the world own just under 90% of the wealth
that exists.

Notes

Benjamin's Fools

In the words of the clan of Wu
Cash Rules Everything Around Me and you
It's King Cash that dictates the rule
The one by which you choose to live
The one that dictates how much you would be
  willing to give
Of yourself and what you will compromise
Against your principles so you can live the
  lies
Global society based on the Benjamins
Distorting the truth so we all live in sins
Dollar Dollar bills that you worship
Making you deny your own truth — can it
  really be worth it?
Mind and bodies sold like in prostitution
How are you any different when you're in
  collusion
When you say nothing and choose silence
Pretending to be blind so you don't notice
  the violence
As they kill anyone where there's an oil
  field
You really think they care about the God to
  who you kneel?
Refer to mass murder as collateral damage
Justifications of the lands they ravage
Chase and overtake until it's all gone
At this rate that time ain't gonna be long
Scheme and scam immoral attackers
You seem to forget who is The Best of all
  Planners
He who watches and takes note of the
  falsities we praise

Notes

He to whom we will answer at the end of our
   days
So be mindful of the choices you make
Choose what's right for your own sake
And not just for you but what's good for all
For living just for yourself makes you
   simply a fool...
And in the words of brother Tupac Shakur
'They got money for war, but they can't feed
   the poor'
And from the very beginning it wasn't our war
The lie of the media who knocks on our door
While the rich sit back and lay down the law
Telling the rest of us how we should live
All the while there's no money to give
To all the people that are most in need
Yet all the while corruption to feed their
   greed
Anyone an enemy from a foreign land
Why can't we reach out instead to give a
   helping hand? Apparently, we should fear a
   terrorist invasion
Apparently, we are the innocent nation
Apparently, war is our own salvation
And all the while we plant the seed
Paranoid masses to feed our greed
When will the destruction ever end?
Will we with our conscience ever make
   amends?
And through this conscience, will we ever
   stand up
And demand to cry out enough is enough?
For it is not enough to silently pray
For a better day to come our way
Our collective humanity demands a solution
A path to peace — a revolution...

Notes

It is generally estimated there are at any one point around 40 million victims of modern slavery — human trafficking around the globe.

Notes

Souled Out

You forcibly moved me from my place of birth
Displacing my safety, to take me around the
  earth
Taking away my opportunity
Valuing me no more than the lowest form of
  commodity
Selling my body, whilst you sold your own
  soul
Human Traffic your capitalist goal
You divided the earth so unequally
Taking all for yourself, leaving nothing for
  me
To the point where I had to search so
  desperately
For any means just to survive and live
Even it meant my body was yours to give
To others who cared not and would do as they
  please
Raping me of my dignity and leaving me on my
  knees
And to all those that judge
I pray you're never in my desperate
  situation
Nations and generations
Victims of mass manipulation
The result of colonial mentality and seizing
  of wealth
Taking what was ours to keep it all for
  yourself
Cycles of slavery repeating themselves
Until we are seen as equals, nothing will
  ever change
Desperation and death will always remain
Bodies in lorries and in the seas

Notes

With your consumption mentality there will
   be no reprieve
My situation is not so far from your own
But until you acknowledge we are one, I will
   remain alone...
And for the savagery of humankind
I was sold
A child, a boy, not yet a man
Sold. In a way most underhand
One of millions of stories, forgotten and
   untold
A child, a girl, not yet a woman
A living testimony to how morality has
   fallen
I was sold
My story is not new, but one of old
Serving humankind's appetite of lusts
   uncontrolled
Where is your love and where is your care?
Broken promises of all those that claimed
   they would 'always be there'
An apparent shame of society, something
   incorrect
My innocence abandoned, to a point of
   neglect
And apparently, I was part of tomorrow's
   hope,
Remember, humankind, you reap what you sow
Trafficked and owned
I was sold.
No safe area for me, my life a war zone
Betrayed and commodified, all alone.
Your need for consumption
The real root of my destruction
You cannot see the connection
Therein the route of my rejection

Notes

Not part of your reality
Is it that you refuse to see?
Or that you turn away from me, more
  accurately?
And for that very act of your savagery...
I. Was. Sold.

Notes

Facts of Attacks

Weapons of mass distraction
To cause hysteria reaction
Mass media in collusion
To reinforce the illusion
Predictable calamity
Carefully constructed fallacy
Government would never do that?
What's that — sell you lies as a fact?
Cycles of terror
Dividing people forever
Security forces critical code
Paranoid panic overload
Are we really meant to believe?
Mr Terrorist waits for the right moment
  politically?
That he times his attacks conveniently
At just the right moment strategically
Innocent lives taken as collateral
Damage on repetition until it becomes
  natural
Not sayin' these terrorists ain't for real
Simply asking who's behind it all?

Notes

White Wash

You, you whitewashed my history
Made me all about savagery
Then claimed you brought me civility
As if I had no ability
As if it wasn't enough that you imposed your
  slavery
Through your agenda of divide and colony
Your Eurocentric mentality
Rest of the world's fatality
Your belief of being above
Whatever you take, never enough
Oppression on mass human scale
Distorted facts, information fail
You came to my royal land
You came with your stealing hand
No intention to unite
Only to invade and fight
How can you be in the right?
How can you be the one with wealth?
What do you really think when you look at
  yourself?
Is it really me in need of your charity?
Or do the masses need information clarity?
Of how the great empires were made
And from where the foundations were laid?
And we now talk as if they were different times
When in reality you still follow the same line
Of greed and corruption and commodity
  control
No share in any profit as you want it whole
And until this equation changes for real
I will never accept any deal
Your fake claims of the end of the slave
It is your integrity lost that you really
  should save...

Notes

Black Mystery Month

They gave me a month of history
As if that could reflect all of me
And my human connection intricacy
Why am I even acknowledged differently?
Isn't our past simply the story of you and
  me?
And that the month must even exist,
Speaks of the narrative of those who resist
Who refuse to be forgotten in time
Who refuse to simply accept the crime
Of forgetting my multiple contributions
To our way of living and our institutions
Here from the very beginning
There is nowhere they have walked that I
  have not been
My history is their very own story
Yet they separate our pasts to take their
  glory
Modern times treat me like I never had
  nothing to give
Did you hear of King Mansa Musa the richest
  man that ever lived?
My multiplicity of kingdoms that tell the
  story of my past
All the while when they were living in ages
  of dark
And to all those that don't understand my
  relevancy Know: you will never understand
  yourself
Without acknowledging me...

Notes

By Any Means.

Why can't 'they' protest peacefully?
Is your murder of countless young sons,
  daughters, fathers and mothers peaceful?
Is your subjugation and multiple examples of
  oppression peaceful?
Is your raping of lands, dealings underhand,
  pillaging and criminal profiling of one race
  against another peaceful?
Is your foot on the neck of your victim
  peaceful?
Did you find the cries of the human being
  underneath your knee of slow suffocation
  pleading 'I can't breathe' whilst you
  continued to press down peaceful?
Were your looting & shooting of countless
  indigenous communities peaceful?
Is your system of appropriation of
  everything from 'minority ethnic' cultures
  & communities whilst presenting us as basic
  & savage peaceful?
Understand your violence.
Your violence of privilege.
Wherein you have created a circumstance that
  entitles you to more of this one world,
  simply because of the tone of your flesh.
Your violence. Where you have intoxicated
  human psychologies into believing your
  colour is in some way more pure & better.
Your violence. Where you believe your life
  is of more worth and that justifies the
  taking of multiples of lives under the term
  collateral damage across the world.
Your violence. That has systematically, over
  centuries, had the specific agenda to take

Notes

and dominate and misappropriate all interpretations of & access to wealth & its distribution.

Your violence. Where you have reinterpreted history to intentionally make our histories unknown and a mystery, whilst falsely proposing it is you that gave us civilisation through your great nations.

Your violence. When I tell you Black Lives Matter and you arrogantly and belligerently respond with 'All lives Matter'.

Your violence. Where you speak up against the burning of buildings in protest, yet you have remained silent on countless people being killed by the knees of those very authorities that are paid to protect us all.

Your violence. Where you chastise anyone that takes a knee for his own dignity and that of his whole community, restricting his access to work in order to suppress his character, message of conscience and income.

Your violence. Wherein you silence our voices of resistance and reinterpret them as voices of extremism.

Your violence. Wherein you presented to the rest of the world, a royal continent, with more emperors, kings & queens that you knew exactly all about, stripped it of its resources & portrayed it as enslaved and impoverished.

Your violence. Where, because of the colour of their skin a person cannot go for a walk, a run, sit in their car, go shopping, take a walk into a neighbourhood, simply

Notes

just breathe & live in peace. Every.
Single. Day.
Why don't 'they' protest peacefully?
Why do you still see them as 'they' & not as
    'we' for only when we all stand up against
    racist hatred & oppression will anybody
    truly be free.
Protest peacefully?
When violence is the strategy of the enemy?
Then in the words of brother Malcolm,
    protest, 'by any means necessary'.
In order for real change to happen it must be
    institutional from the very top, those
    power structures that have created,
    reinforced & perpetuated mentalities of
    division, 'the other', justified brutality,
    supremacy & inhumanity, must be dismantled
    to allow the opportunity for new structures
    & systems to be built, based on the
    recognition of universal equality,
    opportunity & freedoms for all people.
In order for real change to happen it must be
    personal growing from our deepest roots,
    our perspectives & the thought processes
    that lead us there, our psychologies of
    processing, understanding & feeling of both
    the past and present and future pathways to
    increase the opportunity for new & better
    possibilities.
We cannot simply 'keep calm & carry on',
    witnessing & accepting the inequalities
    that are prevalent & relevant, to each &
    every one of us, contaminating our
    societies & our psychologies.
We cannot remain silent. We must protest. We
    must speak up as if the injustice we

Notes

witness against others is to our very own family, because it actually is - IF you truly accept & embrace that we are all part of one human family.

Protest. Protest through our personal interpretations & reflections, our interactions & conversations, at every & any given point, until what we perceive and are willing to accept as our collective normality is truly different from what has gone before.

Only at this point will we have a chance at least for a better tomorrow for us all.

Notes

Family Frustrations: Afternoon

Ramadan Prep Conversations:

Me: This year, fasting is exceptionally long, so we must pace ourselves in whatever we do.

Dad: Yes, the TV should be off for the month.

Mum: What does the TV have to do with anything?

Dad: Don't get touchy just because you can't watch your dramas.

Mum: Where does it say when you're fasting you can't watch TV? I didn't know I was married to the Imam who set the rules.

Dad: Well, obviously it wouldn't say that as TVs weren't invented then.

Mum: So, you're adding in YOUR own rules then, aren't you? Maybe you should worry about having to answer for that shouldn't you, rather than telling me about watching my dramas and causing them.

Dad: I'm just saying it for your benefit, so you think of Allah.

Mum: Don't you worry — I think of Allah every time I look at you, even when I'm not fasting.

Dad: Yeah? You too, yeah?

Me: Anyways, like I said, we need to pace ourselves...

Ramadan Conversations:

Me: I'll make the tea for everyone.

Mum: That's OK, I'm doing it.

Me: OK, thank you, Mum, but can you please put the honey in my tea this time?

Mum: You're being ungrateful.

Me: No, I am thankful. I'm just saying if you offer to make tea for someone you make it to their preference, not the way you think they should have it.

Mum: Well, I'm teaching you the proper way to have it, it's not my fault that you don't know at your age — do you hear me complaining when you make the tea? No, you don't.

Me: That's because I make your tea how you like it to be done, besides there's no proper or wrong, it's just individual taste. After fasting all day, everyone should have tea just how they like?

Mum: Well after fasting all day a son shouldn't do his mum's head in, especially when she is still putting in the effort to try and teach him how to tea properly at his big age.

Me: Right. OK, thank you.

Dad: Why does my phone keep telling me to update all the time, son?

Me: It means the software needs updating, Dad, you need to leave it on charge overnight.

Dad: Yeah, why does it keep saying it every night then?

Me: Just because you charge it at night, doesn't mean it's updating; we need to press the update button.

Dad: Well, I'm happy with my phone, I don't need to be updated about another one.

Me: No, it will still be the same phone, Dad, that's upgrade when they give you a newer one.

Dad: Update. Upgrade. You sort it and tell them from me they can't tell me any new news I don't already know that I need to know.

Me: Right. OK, Dad...

Mum: Aleeksa Aleeksa.

Me: Erm... Mum... what are you doing?

Mum: She's very naughty, she's not saying anything is she?

Me: Who's naughty?

Mum: What, are your ears not working or something? You can hear I'm talking to Aleeksa!

Me: Ohhhh, Alexa!

Mum: That's what I've been saying, haven't I? What's wrong with you? Anyways, tell her to play Beauty on the Beach.

Me: Play what?

Mum: What's up with you? Beauty. On. The. Beach? What's the issue? You know the cartoon I'm talking about.

Me: You mean Beauty and the Beast?

Mum: Don't try and act clever with your pronunciation — think you're too Englizi these days just tell her to play it.

Me: It's not pronunciation; it's two different words Beach and Beast.

Mum: Yeah, that's what I said?

Me: No, it's two words, Mum — You know what, I'm sorry, yes, I'll tell 'her' to play it...

Mum: Tell her to behave too and listen to me in the first place.

Me: Right, OK, I'll make sure to tell her...

Me: You should take those sweets to Bangladesh.

Mum: No, it's too hot they will get sticker.

Me: It's not sticker.

Mum: Yes, I know it's not sticker here, I'm talking about Bangladesh.

Me: No, I mean the word, it's not sticker, it's 'sticky'.

Mum: That's what I said.

Me: No, Mum, sticky — 'eee'.

Mum: Yes, I'm saying stickerrrr!

Dad: Don't worry, her two-year-old granddaughter will be here soon — she can teach her...

Me: Here's your tea...

Dad: Have you seen the state of your hair?

Me: The phrase is 'thank you'.

Dad: Thank you for what, our son looking like a hippy?

Me: For the tea.

Dad: What about it?

Me: Thank you.

Dad: You're welcome, son, you can make it anytime for us — only when we want it though — do I really have to tell you about the state of your hair at your age?

Me: No, you don't, as I think how I look is up to me.

Dad: I'm just trying to help you, son — honestly, why don't you do something right in your life — at least you could start with your hair.

Mum: He probably does it on purpose, so he won't get a wife.

Me: OK, thank you — same time tomorrow?

Mum: Do we have to tell you every day?

Eid Day Conversation:

(kettle already boiling)

Me: Ahh you making the teas then dad?

Dad: Do I look like your tea boy?

Me: No I was just saying since you had the kettle boiling

Dad: Yeah I'm being considerate to you and helping you along

Me: So you want me to make the tea as always

Dad: It's Eid I'm giving you a purpose.

Me: What so do I look like your tea boy then?

Dad: Doesn't matter what you look like son - you are my tea boy.

Corona Conversations:

Dad: I heard with the Corona Virus you shouldn't let your throat go dry — would you like a tea, son?

Me: Aw, yes please then, Dad.

Dad: Well, what are you waiting for then? It's not going to make itself is it? Make your mum and me one whilst you're at it.

Me: So, you want me to make you a tea?

Dad: I shouldn't have to tell you — all this explaining could make my throat dry, son.

Me: I was reading an article that confirmed squatting is the best way to go to the toilet.

Dad: Well, don't start squatting on the toilet seat because if you fall in, I'm not coming in there to get you out.

Me: I'm not talking about squatting on the toilet seat I'm just saying I was reading so maybe we could get a step?

Mum: A step? Here we go again...

Me: I'm just sayin'...

Mum: Why do you have to always say? OK, let's get a step, yeah? Why don't you get a whole staircase and bannister in there while you're at it?

Dad: Well, at least that means it's very unlikely he would fall in...

Me: No one is going to fall in, Dad!

Deeper Introspections 2

Whilst our sins can be 'counted' hence our accountability for our actions, our blessings are 'countless', in that for just a single action, the blessings it is possible to receive may be multiplied over and again to such a degree that even the angels cannot quantify... Such is the love and mercy of the Creator...

Notes

Despite the facade of my outward persona, often it is difficult to believe things can and will be better, to really know there can be something better than what is apparent in the now and to strive to make it so... More so, it's easier to simply write it all off and act accordingly, even dare I say, to be part of the destruction of any possibility myself. Part of the difficulty of allowing ourselves to really believe and have faith, I guess, is that it requires a level of vulnerability and exposure of our inner workings, and in a world that is based on a self-assured approach, where everything is positioned and placed into labels and categories to identify and support our understanding, accepting and even embracing there are possibilities beyond that which we can comprehend and ever understand, is a position that would seem to be in direct contradiction, and perhaps this is part of the very point.

Notes

The instances of human experiences where outcomes have been beyond that which anyone could comprehend are in multiples, beyond even our ability to collate, both in our personal experiences and upon really looking at the evolvement of our collective human history. To be open to the possibilities of the miracles of life is a form of emancipation that allows us to live beyond our personal psychological prisons and live in a state of actual freedom and love...

Notes

In as much as we revere and celebrate our days of independence and the apparent individuality of our identities of nationhood, perhaps we should all collectively celebrate a global day of interdependence, wherein we reach out to one another, celebrating our connections and similarities, for surely they are many more in number then the differences we allude to?

Notes

'And whomsoever removes the obstacles in the path of another receives the blessings of the Creator'* ...Without exception, we all have obstacles of varying natures to overcome. Indeed, in some instances, beyond the literal obstacles that are apparent, our perceptions and those entities that influence them are part of the barriers that prevent and diminish the possibilities of our progress. Let us each endeavour to remove and overcome the obstacles we personally face, in order that we may reach out to one another, to encourage rather than discourage, to comfort and alleviate discomfort, removing the obstacles we each individually face in our personal struggles of life, in order that we may all collectively move forward in the most blessed of beautiful paths...

*Taken from the verified sources of the quotes of the holy prophet Muhammed (peace be upon him).

Notes

Maybe it is not meant to be made easier, maybe the resilience we need to live through the process and all we suffer and endure is part of it, failing and knowing it wasn't and isn't the end, the self-doubt, the questioning of what the point is starting all over again each and every time. Not because we know any better that this new time will work, but just because we can and because we can, we try, maybe the failures in themselves are part of the very point so that we may understand humility and appreciation in the rare instances of our personal successes when they come. For surely, they will. For each and every one of us.

Notes

And if we are each no more than travellers in this lifetime, warned against worldly attachments, then surely those who call out to our hearts are connections that transcend what we merely are able to think and know, understood only through love itself and only by the soul...

Notes

And what if, simply, we just believed in one another? Encouraged and reassured and were there, wherein we each believed we were collectively more than what we could ever possibly dare to believe we could be alone? What then?

Notes

Dignity and pride are often perceived as convoluted cousins, mistaken in identity indicative of how closely they are related. However, upon deeper reflection, the difference between them is both clear and distinct. Whilst pride is often the cause of looking down on others with arrogance, dignity invariably aligns itself with humility, indeed to dignify oneself and to dignify others is to elevate our interactions to realms of respect, reaching out in understanding far beyond any pride would ever permit...

Notes

The notion of 'Sabr' or patience in Islam is deemed so significant that it was described by the prophet, peace be upon him, as being attributable to one half of a person's faith (the other being 'Shukr' or appreciation). While I am open about my lack of knowledge on most issues and in particular my Islamic knowledge, I am continuously endeared towards the beauty of its nuance. Each of our daily lives, regardless of a faith (or non) affiliation are filled with constant reminders of our need for patience, for perseverance to endure our momentary scenarios and situations in order to reach a greater goal. The notion of accepting Sabr is to persist in our efforts without worry, thereby negating and releasing the stress we often each feel in its various forms in modern-day lives. To demonstrate patience, in effect, not through ignoring our personal frustrations, rather, through the contentment of the grace of one's faith.

Notes

Social Commentary 2

The hatred of the human race of itself is, without doubt, the saddest indictment of our claim to compassion and love. An inability to hold to account our self-humiliation through our destructive obsession with political nuance. We continue to enslave one another, physically seemingly unable to make the connection to our own psychological and spiritual emancipation. Stealing instead of sharing, one dominant culture over the other, appropriation manifesting in identities stolen, the disparity of our values of lives a downward scale based on the hues of our flesh. So far have we travelled down our paths of manipulation and destruction of peoples across the world, no longer do we even recognise our own genocide. Our international relations a reflection of no unity of nations, instead minority agendas of conquer and divide...

Notes

Profilic Colours

What colour should my profile picture be?
To reflect accurately and ever so adequately
The level of inequality and disparity
We view tragedy and inhumanity
What colour can reflect the pain and
  suffering?
The lost generations we view with arrogant
  indignation
Whose pain we dismiss as mere sensationalism
Supposedly different from me and you
Simply because they are the wrong colour hue
What colour is the shade of our arrogant
  discrimination?
That turns victim situations into ones of
  criminalisation.
A blind eye to rape and murder whatever the
  cost
A real reflection on how far we are lost
And while we can never blame the blind for
  not being able to see
What of those who turn away just because
  'it's all too much for me'?
Speak up, shout out for what you know is just
  wrong
This is the only path to justice and to know
  we belong
To one another, living with security
The only way to ensure we all are free...

Notes

Amongst the most enduring of freedom struggles is that of the people of Palestine who have had to endure systematic rape, torture and murder at the hands of their oppressors all the while having their homes and lands illegally stolen and annexed.

Supported by luminaries including Albert Einstein, Nelson Mandela, Gandhi, Che Guevara, Malcolm X, amongst many, many others, the voices for liberty and freedom continue to resist the powers that seek to silence them.

Notes

Intifada

Uprise against the disaster
Stand up to the colonial master
The more you oppress, we fight harder
Nablus to Ramallah
Tryna take away our legitimacy
Destroy our documented history
Land divided with your hypocrisy
Know that every one of our people stands
    strong
Understand that we will always know we
    belong
Even if the world pretends not to listen
We live to fight the system
We exist to resist
Insist, on our freedom, liberty
The system.
That uproots the olive tree
That strips away our liberty
That caused 'the catastrophe'
That repeats itself on the very anniversary
The system
That takes away our worth
Decides we have no place on earth
That makes us the terrorist
Simply because we want to exist
The system
The cause of the destruction
The root of corruption
That created the Balfour Treaty
That inflicts its deadly weaponry
That kills Laila the baby
The system
That underestimates you and me
Better know we don't stand for its fuckery

Notes

That does not account for our collective
  humanity
That does not understand our united dignity
- Knowing we will never ever rest until
  Palestine is truly recognised as a reality

Notes

It is estimated that around 1 million Uyghur peoples of China are being, or have been held at some point, in modern-day concentration camps by Chinese government authorities, with the aim of forcefully 're-educating' them away from their faith beliefs. The world, by and large, stays silent.

Notes

Memoirs of a Uyghur

And where are all the people that said,
  'Never again would we allow...?'
Where are all those people now?
Existing in a way upon us that is forced
Do you fail to see the signs of holocaust?
Labelled, consigned and concentrated
My own way of living means I'm incarcerated
A million of my people being re-educated
Death agenda to my faith dedicated
Controversy to raise my issues of my freedom
Would it be another way if I was a different
  religion?
Manipulate to indoctrinate
My fate a result of hate
When will the world speak for me?
When will they stand up collectively?
When they finally decide, will it be too
  late?
Are my rights and my plight only heard by the
  deaf?
Or is it that the world will wait until of my
  people nothing is left?
Delusions of Muslim ummah unity
Where are they now then to come save me?
I suppose I am just part of another minority
Suppressed and oppressed
And forgotten conveniently
My request for my rights
Just not worth the fight
Just another Diary of a Muslim Nobody...
In the mid 90's it is estimated over 8000
  Bosniak males, both men and boys were
  massacred and a further 20000 women and
  children expelled from their lands, on the

Notes

basis of their faith with the agenda of
'ethnic cleansing.' The United Nations
failed to intervene watching helplessly as
these crimes on humanity happened on what
they had previously deemed 'a safe area'.

Notes

Srebrenica

The earth knows our secrets
No matter the publicity we avoid
It knows all we destroyed
It bears witness to the destruction
Committed only upon human instruction
The earth knows our secrets
Blood drenched soil
To our own humanity disloyal
Apparent differences between us
Enough for us to act in distrust
Enough for us to commit acts of disgust
Mass murder
Over and over
The dirtiest of actions under the guise of
  'cleansing'
The most polluted of psychology
Indoctrination threatening
Constant message of hating the other
Ensuring our empathy is left to suffer
Lives once lived now forgotten
Simply bodies in the soil until they go
  rotten
The earth knows all our secrets

Notes

Passing Points...

And there came a point in time where the
  world became so deluded
The truth became a distant memory
Lies accepted and embraced
In almost every single case
And the everyday people accepted and
  colluded
No questioning of morality
No care for the potential calamity
Of millions more lives murdered
As the truth was merely distorted further
Such was humankind's detachment from its own
  humanity
And the scriptures described the very times
Where people themselves would simply accept
  the crime
Their hearts sealed against the divine
  decree that to even kill one was to kill
  all humanity
Unable to see the link between their mockery
  of war and Insaan's* insanity
And there came a point in time where good
  people mocked
No longer shocked
Upon knowing the potential for more war
  would mean death and destitution
Such was their delusion
At the potential of hope to believe it could
  be better
More than could, that it should
Such was their detachment
They no longer carried any attachment
To any sense of responsibility
Resigned to the so-called 'powers that be'

Notes

And their destruction monopoly
There actually came a point in time where
  this was the very case
Within the very masses of the human race
Where such was its obsession with self
It no longer could distinguish between money
  and wealth
And for personal popularity and simple
  satisfaction
It would joke about the most evil of acts,
  just for a reaction
On social media and their newsfeed
Obsessed only with 'likes' to feed its greed
The thing is 'it' is you and I
And it is not a compulsion to believe in the
  lie
We do not have to be complicit and simply
  watch another time pass by
As more of humanity at our own hands die
Against each and every immorality we will
  stand up
For justice and peace, nothing is too much
Obsession with love is our only way
To let go of this hope is too much to pay
A price that is beyond what we could ever
  afford
Surely one day we will answer to our Lord
And on that day what will any of us say?
When He questions us on why we turned away?

*Insaan are humankind translated from the
Arabic.

Notes

The current threat to the environment around the world, perhaps most tragically symbolised through the brazen destruction of the Amazon rainforest for monetary profit, is reaching the point of no return according to many environmentalists and researchers. Once lost, the impact on the earth's ecosystem will be undeniable and possibly catastrophic. It is up to each of us to act now in order to ensure there is actually a tomorrow for future generations.

Notes

Consumption Destruction...

Consumption destruction
Earth under eruption
Life under implosion
Care under erosion
Ever a need
To feed our greed
Air, land and sea
All victim fatality
We continue to kill
Murderers for real
And we have the nerve
To think it's all here to serve
Simply our way of life
Our toxicity is rife
Human-unkind
To any life we find
Polluting the earth
Undervalue its worth
Disregard the love it deserves
Simply to serve THE NEED FOR now
Never ending pollution
Without any solution
Environmental catastrophe
Indictment on our collective inhumanity
And as slowly we can no longer breathe
Maybe then we will see clearly
It is we that should live humbly
It is Mother Earth that is greater than us
And we owe to her not to break her trust...
As she cries 'with your fires of finance, you
  burned me!'
Your flames set intentionally
Your arrogant dismissal of your need
Motivated and set by your greed

Notes

And while it is me that cannot breathe
Wait and see when I leave
A message beyond simply the trees and the
  leaves
For then there will be no reprieve
Clearing me away from your land
So that you can implement your plans
Growing cash crops
Money motivation never stops
Ancient knowledge dismissed
Benjamin's too hard to resist
Over obsession with meat consumption
Gluttony always leads to destruction
Disregarding all the life of the region
No care for the ecosystem weakened
Ancient tribes fight to keep me alive
Humility to nature and hear my cry
While you're concerned with what you can
  take
Problem is no matter how much money you all
  make
No good when you all suffocate
After killing me and all that call me home
You find it's yourselves you have destroyed
  and now alone
And when by then it will all be too late
For then you will all have sealed your fate
You see I am an essential part of this earth
Like many things, when I'm gone, you'll
  finally realise my true worth
Oh, Human Race with your poisonous waste
Your toxic plastic
Situation now drastic
Dare you deny the warming? Refuse to heed my
  warning?
Suffocating me with your industrial fumes

Notes

No regard for the danger that looms
For my lands as the seas rise
For the extinction of my animals as they
  continue to die
At the mercenary hands of your greed
As you service your wants not just your
  needs
There was a time we lived in harmony
There was a time when you saw the value of me
Held me in reverence as Mother Earth
And now you seem to no longer value my worth
And now you seem to possess little value for
  nature
Or, what little you have, your arrogance
  seems greater
A planet and people that once were great
Now consumed with consumption not concerned
  with its fate
A disregard for the stories of what came
  before
Of what happened to those that looked down
  upon nature's law
For many times many great nations have
  fallen
Every time when they have been
  self-absorbing
With no care or concern for what was around
  them
No humility in living and just want allowed
  them
When will the cycle of destruction stop?
When the fields are so poisoned and there is
  nothing to crop?
Is that when you will hang your heads in
  shame?
Realising only when nothing remains?

Notes

When the arrogance of man's consumption
Leads to the point where you can no longer
  function?
Then finally will you lament?
On how you murdered your surroundings and
  environment...

Notes

We Without Territory

We are people with no land
A forgotten community with no helping hand
Our territory destroyed by environmental
  destruction
If you look further, you will find human
  consumption
At the very source of our suffering and
  destruction
Globalisation and economic instruction
The plants and animals already started to
  perish
All that we should be holding dear and really
  cherish
And now humankind kills even itself
All for the illusion of monetary wealth
Keep on chasing until you can't recognise
  yourself
We are the people with no land
Our stability as stable as sand
Forgotten and remote so no one can see
Our suffering will never make viral mass tv
We lived in harmony with the ecological
  system
Once destroyed no chance for remission
And by the time you realise, it will be too
  late
Nature's revenge our sealed fate
How will you answer God when you are asked?
About your accountabilities for all that has
  passed?
About how you saw, but chose to be blind?
About your washing of hands, rather than
  choosing to be kind?

Notes

About you simply saying it's 'not down to
   me'
'I can't change things personally'
About the fact you diminish your
   responsibility?
We are the people with no land
Forgotten communities of the earth
With no helping hand...

Notes

Community Corona

And eventually science fiction
Became a true depiction
Of how life was to become
Not just for the characters in those
   futuristic stories but, for everyone
The 'beam me up' intercoms
Now mobile phones
Talking ourselves into networks of dual
   reality
Plugged into multiple matrixes seen as
   normality
And once seen as only science fantasy
All the while big brother watched
Every move clocked
In our Brave New World
Under the guise of security
No questions asked on the corporate guards
Watching over you and watching over me
Control, confuse and regulate
Systems of oppressive hate
And before the fiction stories of not so long
   ago
When you go back to ancient prophesy
   foretold
There are multiple stories of old
Describing how societies set about their
   implosion
Caused by their ethical corrosion
This is not any new story
Simply study the tales of history
Many people believed they were the best
Thought they were beyond the Creator's test
When they saw the suffering of others turned
   away

Notes

Remained silent as long 'they were kept at
  bay'
And a single moment was all it took
For their world and their life to be shook
You really think the killer virus is
  Covid-19?
What about how you killed your own humanity?
Labelling others as immigrants and refugees
Now witness people fight for toiletries
Our so-called civilised society
Will you now live with humility?
And no matter how much you hand sanitise
Won't clean away your filth and lies
The virus of divide and hate
The virus that made you manipulate
The virus where you commodified
The virus where you sold your lies
The virus of inequality
That made people look at one another
  indifferently.
Another story
From the laboratory
Population out of control
System of finance overload
Panic buying
As if you're dying
Tomorrow we'll discuss a new disease
That could bring the world to its knees
No one knows what to do?
Maybe watch The Simpsons to get a clue?
Let's start by talking about how to fix
  ourselves
Start understanding what is true wealth
The very same truth since time begun
The fact we're all meant to live as one
The fact we all have the same fragility

Notes

The fact we should be living in unity
And while humanity believed it had been
  somehow suffocated
The places human beings had now vacated
Were in fact actually liberated
The waters that for so long had been polluted
Were now cleaned up and undiluted
And the air that for so long had been
  suffocated
Would invite us to take a new breath
One to signify a new life, in fact, far from
  death
And the earth was allowed to live
Now, if only humanity was to truly look
  after itself
Share its resources and fairly distribute
  its wealth
If humanity could only live together through
  this terrible moment
Live for one another and seek atonement
For the selfish way we had lived previously
And now live for each other unselfishly
Including all in between young and elderly
Shared strength to those with vulnerability
Then, this would be a moment of collective
  community
A chance to transform to a different norm
And a way of life would begin that was always
  meant to be...

Notes

Family Frustrations: Evening

Dad: Boy, when you shower in this house, I told you to wipe the tiles after.

Me: Yeah, sorry, Dad, I forgot.

Dad: Well, you don't forget to wipe yourself, do you?

Me: The tiles are waterproof anyway, Dad, so it doesn't really matter.

Mum: So, you didn't forget, you just didn't bother is what you really mean.

Me: No, I'm just sayin'...

Dad: We know what you are saying, son, don't you worry... Don't even know why you bother showering every day anyway as if you're Mr Clean... we've seen your clothes all over the floor...

Me: OK, thanks, would you like a cup of tea?

Dad: Make it then and make sure the cups are clean, don't start telling us there's no need as they're 'waterproof'.

Mother's Day Conversations:

Me: 'Happy Mother's Day!'

Mum: Every day is Mother's Day, son.

Me: I know, but today is extra special, everything you want you shall have — what would you like?

Mum: You have done enough already. The tea you made was better than usual.

Me: Wait, Mum, so you are saying you normally don't like my tea?

Mum: No, I'm saying today you must have given it the Mother's Day touch.

Me: I make it the same way for you every day though?

Mum: See, son, like I said every day is Mother's Day — you are getting quicker at picking things up lately — better late than never — maybe you will soon be able to pick up a wife after all...

Ramadan Conversations:

Mum: What exactly are you doing?

Dad: Preparing.

Mum: Preparing what?

Dad: Preparing the potatoes.

Mum: Preparing them for what?

Dad: Well, you know we are fasting, so I'm preparing them for Iftar so we are ready to open the fast.

Mum: But there's still over six hours to go why do you need to do this now?

Dad: You just sit there on that armchair of yours and do what you're doing, don't worry about me.

Mum: Oh, here we go...

Dad: That's right not here we go, here we've gone... you do your Allah Allah

Mum: I will do my Allah Allah, don't you worry...

Dad: I'm not worried... If I don't prepare things in this house, then who will?

Mum: And there it is... you only ever prepare things so you can ask your special question!

Dad: That's right I will ask, really, I don't need to ask as there's only ever one answer...

Mum: But you still keep asking...

Dad: Oh, for God-sakes, is it raining outside again?!

Me: Well, actually, Dad, it isn't going to be raining inside is it? Besides it's a blessing for it to rain as it washes away the sins of the world, so you shouldn't say God-sakes.

Dad: Don't get smart with me, son. I told you it doesn't suit you and that's what I meant for the sake of God Alhumdulilah for the rain.

Me: No, that's not what you meant, and now you are lying on top of that.

Dad: Boy, I'm lying? Don't worry about my lies, and if the rain washes sins away, you better go stand outside and get real wet as I know what you get up to.

Dad: Why don't you have some coleslaw?

Me: I've told you, Dad, every time you keep asking me, I don't like it.

Dad: Why not?

Me: Just that's my taste — you and Mum can have it.

Dad: So, you're trying to say you have better taste then your mum and dad?

Me: No, I'm just saying I personally don't want any coleslaw with my food.

Dad: Doesn't make any sense. It tastes nice.

Me: Yeah, that's nice for you. If it tastes nice, you can have more if I don't have it.

Dad: But we are sharing it with you, and now you are trying to say your taste is better than ours — that's not nice is it, son?

Me: OK, I tell you what, why don't I have some coleslaw on the side?

Dad: See, son? I told you you would like it... I really never understand why you don't just listen to me in the first place...

Indeed.

Me: Dad, you should use this vegan organic coconut butter.

Dad: Why?

Me: It's all-natural ingredients and still tastes nice.

Dad: OK, but the one I use already tastes nice?

Me: But this is made with real ingredients.

Dad: Well, so is my one, it's real, it's not make-believe is it?

Me: No, I mean like natural.

Dad: Do you 'naturally' have to still pay for it at the check-out?

Me: Yeah, it might cost slightly more, but it has only the essential natural ingredients.

Dad: Yeah, don't worry, I will stick to my one, thanks. Trying to get me to pay double for less ingredients, son? Yeah, that makes a lot of sense!

Me: But the extra stuff in yours isn't good for you.

Dad: A little bit of what isn't good for you, is sometimes good for you, son. This is why sometimes I listen to you.

Me: So why don't you listen to me now then?

Dad: I said sometimes — this isn't one of those times, boy. Can't have you getting all carried away with yourself...

OK.

Mum: The grass looks like it needs cutting.

Dad: Well, you haven't got time to do it now as you have to go to work.

Mum: Yes, I know that — that's why I'm telling you — you're home all day.

Dad: Well, the man in the shop told me the new lawnmower works better with a woman's touch.

Mum: Accha? What else did he tell you?

Dad: He said the best time of day to cut grass is when your wife gets home from work.

Mum: See you — you have too many conversations.

Dad: I'm just talking about what's best.

Mum: Yes, that's so considerate.

Dad: I know. Lucky woman you are.

Me: I had my review and meeting at work yesterday.

Dad: Really? What did they say?

Me: They told me they loved my input so far and loved what I had to say.

Mum: Well at least somebody loves you, son.

Erm. Thanks, Mum.

Mum: So, when we were all young, the village land was as far as you could see.

Dad: Here we go, we've been fasting all day he doesn't need to hear all this.

Mum: I'm teaching him about some family history, he's not going to get it from you, is he? You lot didn't know if you're coming or going! At least we had education!

Dad: Coming or going? Well I came and got you, didn't I? And all that education didn't stop your family from believing all the rubbish I told them to give you away and get you over here!

Mum: No, they let me come as they knew you needed help in life.

Dad: Yeah.

Mum: Yeah.

Corona Conversations:

Me: I'm gonna start jogging as part of the daily hour allowed for exercise.

Dad: Yeah, I told your mum to run up the stairs.

Me: That's good — you should both run up and down the stairs.

Dad: No, I didn't say come back down — better she runs all the way up to the attic and stays there, and I stay as far away down here as possible, son. This would be best for everyone's health.

Mum: I can hear you!

Dad: We're just discussing ways to stay healthy…

Deeper Introspections 3

Our kindness will cost, contrary to what we are told, and so will our empathy, love, care and compassion. Furthermore, not only will they cost, they will be at a great expense to all those who choose to indulge in such feelings. Our arrogance, hate, ambivalence, judgement and ignorance will all undoubtedly have to be sacrificed to such a point they will no longer exist when each of us reaches the very best version of ourselves. So, just as with any other aspect of life, there is a cost to our kindness. But upon just a moment's reflection, that which will invariably be sacrificed to attain and achieve it will always be entirely worth it, to the point where we can conclude, in being kind to others, we are only really being kind to ourselves...

Notes

One can never be emotionally free, whilst
psychologically imprisoned.

Notes

We often travel through life looking for our validations through reaching out to outward entities. Relationships, careers, possessions, qualifications, achievements and goals, each providing us with a reassurance that we are doing 'well'. As we acquire more, the more we desire and as we desire more, the further we reach out without ever searching within ourselves for what our truths may actually be.

The search for success in whatever guise this may take, is always internal, a search of reflections, that in turn leads to a deeper understanding of ourselves, the world around us and indeed our role within it.

In order to find the peace that is the treasure of connecting to our own soul, we need to stop looking for external validations and appreciate that just in the reality of our very existence, our validation has already been affirmed in the most beautiful and blessed way.

Notes

And whilst in the moment, our struggles may weigh heavy upon us, surely, they are ultimately indicative of our growth, living and learning to become more than we were previously, a sign of growth, albeit challenging and difficult, to become more than what we were before...

Notes

You see, the thing is this, one can go through life without helping others, not harming them or wishing them bad, but keeping to oneself and focusing solely on the personal issues and problems that invariably prevail in each of our lives. We can go through life not affording the time to give to others in need and simply having the view that it's just not our problem, but here's the thing: Each and every one of the situations we face, wherein we feel compelled to help and reach out often to the point of our own personal sacrifice, are opportunities of blessings in that we have the chance to reach out and support someone beyond our own personal shortcomings. In this respect, the opportunity to be there for others, in whatever capacity we are able, is in fact an opportunity of blessing with the permission of our Creator, who has per-mitted the scenario wherein one of His own creation seeks the help they need through you. It is indeed entirely our individual choice as to whether we provide that support or not as the case may be. If we don't then, eventually, others will stop asking you for help as you will be perceived as someone that doesn't or won't. They will inevitability find the support they need from others as our Creator will send them to those that will help rather then you, the opportunity of His blessing through our recognition of interde-pendence will be lost and what a sad life that would be indeed...

Notes

The fact that we are each independently responsible for ourselves does not detract from the
fact that we are all collectively responsible
for one another.

Notes

And perhaps to question oneself, and the purpose of one's very existence, isn't the indication of a lack of faith, rather the mark of beginning to embark on the most intimate of journeys and understand what it is really all about. For surely, He invites us to self-doubt and question, knowing He has provided the most beautiful of reassurance through the very best of answers...

Notes

Perhaps it is not 'do good and good will come to you' and more accurately, in doing good, good has already come to you with the permission and blessings of the Creator, who has permitted your heart to recognise our obligation to ourselves and to His creation...

Notes

Social Commentary 3

Weaponised Youth

We armed our young
Before even their life had begun
Armed them with hate and disillusion
Filled them violence and confusion
Strip away every resource
Austerity with no remorse
No budget worthy to save a life
Another dead, another knife
We label simply as 'gang mentality'
Brushing over the humanity tragedy
Blame it on grime, blame it on drill
As if the music they hear creates a reason to
  kill
No opportunity and no job
Capitalist mentality murder and rob
Community relations disengaged
A generation of our youth living in rage
No consideration of real public health
What gives our young confidence and provides
  them with wealth?
A generic system of corrupt mis-education
Biased information to the young population
Case after case of stab on repeat
Media news filled with negative defeat
Where are the stories of our youth success?
Just endless narratives of a society's mess
Violence accepted as the norm
For some a normality since the day they were
  born
And until society stops responsibility
  separation
From ourselves and the new generation
Until we all only see ourselves as one
We all continue to arm our young...

Notes

Possibilities of Equality

They're coming! you cried
Never mentioning how you lied
When you had previously arrived
Landed on their very lands
Gone with your stealing hands
And now you claim 'they steal our jobs'
Never mentioning what you robbed
Centuries of corruption
Death and destruction
Until, fair trading and equality
Was no longer a possibility
The oppressive system of disparity
Leaving only no room for any clarity
Other than somehow that you were owed
For all the death through divisions that you
  sowed
There's no room! you said
After taking their lands and leaving them
  for dead
Turn them away!
Turn them away!
Build a wall, keep them at bay!
'Doesn't matter to me'
As long as it's not me and my family!
A world left torn apart
A world left with no heart
And yet here we all live
With so much to give
To one another's understanding
So rather than focusing on who's landing
On whose bit of land
Let's try to give one another a helping hand
Lift one another so that we collectively
  grow

Notes

Create a better world then we know
Rather than focus on what we see differently
Why not focus on our love and unity?
'We can't afford to — keep them at bay'
In response is what you say
Can we really afford not to?
Is what I say back to you
For when we all finally realize we are all one
A better reality for all of us would have
  begun...

Notes

Working-Class Memoirs

You leave me
Leave to exist in my parallel reality
Mass working-class with no real opportunity
Daring to ask why? — accused of theory of
  conspiracy
You are the minority yet in control of the
  authority
Subjugate the majority whilst holding the
  monopoly
Taking away support from those that cannot
  afford
Inhumane accusations of benefit fraud
Media headlines of being 'on the take'
We are all Daniel Blake
Your policy of universal discreditation
Take away from the poor and ruin the nation
You leave me
Leave me to exist in my parallel reality
Strip away my worth and my sense of dignity
You will say this is just working-class
  mentality
You live in comfort while you impose
  austerity
You. Leave. Me.

Notes

Heard it from Heron...

The revolution is an act of collective
  community consciousness.
The revolution is not to merely sell
  ourselves short through acts of angered
  riots only to be labelled & dismissed
  like animals.
The revolution is to acknowledge the issues
  we are raising of justice & equality,
  humanity & accountability, are fundamental
  to the very existence of civilised society.
The revolution is to realise our concerns
  are real and legitimate,
The revolution is to engage & challenge the
  disengaged attitude of those that live of
  the image of their control over us.
The revolution is to realise, while we were
  told we would not be televised, we are
  aware of the real lies, and we no longer
  accept.
The revolution is to understand the
  injustice perpetrated on any human being
  is a crime upon each and everyone one of
  us, and to decide, we no longer accept.
The revolution starts within each of us,
  knowing a change really is possible,
Revolutionary minds, to break free from our
  societal psychological binds,
Revolutionary thinking, to stop society
  sinking.

Notes

Social De-Construction

You see the thing with social construction
Is that it is not under my instruction
So, based on the principle of equity
How will what you decree
Ever really allow me to just be?
They are your rules
That make us fools
If our biology dictates that we are 99.9%
  the same
Then surely our considered differences are
  divisionary and insane
I have decided, simply I am the colours of
  the earth
Not a simplification, more that I know my own
  worth
I don't want to fight
Simply cause you are white
I don't simply attack
Because I am black
To define the colour of my flesh
Is to condemn me to death
To not allow me to live as myself
To redefine my value and disregard my wealth
Of independence and individuality
My very own passions and humanity
So rather than perpetuate your constructions
I will refuse to follow your instructions
Of defining who and what I should be
As I will create my own reality
And rather than construct, I will continue
  to break through
The ceilings of glass that make me worth
  less then you
And I won't stop until I am free to be me
And we live in a world of real equality...

Notes

Restricted Divisions...

And you got us believing
It was just the glass ceiling
That we had to break through
To prove we were just as good as you
Never told us of the walls that divide us
Isolate and categorise
Look down upon and despise
Simply for not being your version of norm
Having to apologise for how we are born
Fighting for every opportunity
Even then never perceived with equality
And as the ages pass, your disdain takes on
    new complexity
To reinforce the message, you're always more
    worthy
Always worth that little more than me
And as the ages pass and the battle gets
    longer
Know we are not worn down, moreover grow
    stronger
We dare to become more aware and care
Not simply for our own situations
But for that of all our community
Understanding our strength is in our unity
On our own terms not simply your stipulations
And as we create and grow and love our own
    identity
We live and learn what it means to be free
And of the world there are no 1st, 2nd or 3rd
Simply your restrictions of socially
    constructed words
And while there is still much work to be done
Know this, we won't rest until just peace
    applies to everyone...

Notes

Family Frustrations Forever

(Watching a cooking show on TV)

Mum: Well that's a tinned mango, isn't it?

Dad: What are you talking about, woman? We've just watched her talk about and show us the fresh mango?

Mum: Say it nicely.

Dad: What?

Mum: Why are you taking her side? You should be taking my side.

Dad: What sides? There is no side. I'm just saying you're saying she's got tinned mangoes and we have both seen her with fresh mangoes.

Mum: Well where's the skin gone then? Fresh ones have skin, and her ones don't.

Dad: You cut the skin off?!

Mum: What do you mean you cut the skin off? I told you, talk to me nicely. Taking her side. Tell her to cut the skin off for you then.

Dad: But she did cut the skin off?

Mum: That's nice for you both isn't it. Quality Foods has nice mangoes.

Dad: Yes, but the season has gone now.

Mum: She must be getting them from Lidl...

Dad: Yes, I shall get you some tomorrow.

Mum: No, they are expensive there, leave it for now.

Dad: You are worth it, wife.

Mum: You still took her side but OK.

Ramadan Conversations:

Dad: So, son, you seem to have a sleeping problem?

Me: Yes, I can't sleep until way after Suhoor until about 4am.

Dad: Yeah, OK, it was a yes or no answer I was looking for.

Me: Yes?

Dad: OK, good, the solution is to stay up all the way and you be the one to wake us up at the right time so we can sleep in peace.

Me: Well, how does that help my sleeping problem?

Dad: Yeah, son, I haven't got time to have a long convo with you as I'm going to sleep now – your mum's already snoring, so it's going to be hard enough as it is...

Mum: I don't snore.

Dad: It's like sleeping next to an elephant.

Erm... OK.

Me: Mum, what are you doing?

Mum: What does it look like I'm doing?

Me: Well it looks like you're sitting in your armchair with the footrest up watching your soaps with your arms stretched out pointing toward the tv.

Mum: So why you asking then if you can see what I'm doing?

Me: Well, your arms and fingers look a bit strange...

Mum: It's called yoga, you idiot — you wouldn't know.

Me: Erm you're right, Mum, I'm not an expert but I don't think you're meant to do it in your armchair.

Mum: Well, the rest of it would be too much at my age — do what you can — that's what Allah says.

Indeed.

Me: I'm going to the passport office.

Dad: Do you want your birth certificate as you will need to show it, won't you?

Me: What?! All these years I always thought I had lost it!

Dad: No, son, it's not the certificate that's lost, it's you.

Me: Well, why didn't you tell me you had it all this time?

Dad: I keep it safe, don't I, as I have to keep re-reading it every so often to check you are actually my son with all the nonsense you come out with, boy!

Mum: This phone takes up too much battery too quickly.

Me: Well, it isn't from you answering the phone is it? — You must be leaving your apps open.

Mum: Well, you can't really talk about answering the phone, can you?

Me: Well if my mum doesn't answer the phone then obviously the son won't answer, as parents set the example for their children to follow, don't they?

Mum: You should be ashamed even once not to answer your mum's call — what if I died?

Me: But if you died, how would you be calling me?

Dad: He could just meet you straight at Hainault gardens of peace as you only work a couple of stops away.

Me: Dad!

Mum: (Death stare to Dad) See, this is what I have to put up with.

Dad: Well, I'm just saying since no one picks up anyone's calls...

Mum: At my age, I'm really tired of the years of early mornings and working so hard.

Me: At my age, I'm tired of working too.

Mum: (Death Stare) What?

Me: What?

Mum: (Death Stare Continued) Did you just say you're tired of working hard at your age?

Me: Erm... No of course not, Mum, is that what you thought I said? I said I think I should 'try' harder to work even harder at my age not that I'm tired.

Mum: Well, it sounded like you said you're tired of working.

Me: Is that what you thought you heard? Don't be silly, Mum — must be your age affecting your hearing...

Dad: Son, how much longer do you need for your make-up? I need to use the bathroom.

Me: It's called face wash, Dad, not make-up.

Dad: OK, but it's not soap, is it? So, it's make-up.

Me: No. Face wash and make-up are not the same.

Dad: Face wash, yeah? Very fancy, son. You can wash your face as much as you like, you can't wash your face more handsome so just accept 'my dad is better looking than me', now get out the bathroom.

Me: Right. Yes of course, Dad...

Dad: There are some Indian sweets in the fridge. Make sure you eat them.

Mum: Really? I didn't realise they were Indian sweets.

Dad: Well, you wouldn't, would you? Lucky I'm here to tell you once again.

Mum: What do you mean I wouldn't? Besides, I'm not eating anything sweet, so once again what you are telling me is of no use.

Dad: Well, as they say, you are what you eat, so maybe you should try actually listening to what I'm telling you for once and try eating as many as you can — might sweeten up that attitude of yours.

Mum: So, you want our blood pressure and diabetes to get worse?

Dad: After all these years of marriage, my blood pressure really couldn't get worse, so a sweet is the least of my worries!

Dad: Stick some more water in the kettle, son.

Me: There's already a litre in there.

Dad: So? I didn't ask how much was in there, I told you to stick some more in.

Me: But there's already enough, and it will just mean it will take longer to boil and make the tea.

Dad: Boy, haven't you worked it out yet? You are going to be boiling the water and making your dad a tea for as long as we are both alive, so what difference a couple of extra minutes right now gonna make?

Yes. OK.

Me: Mum get the coriander out the bag for me, please.

Mum: But you're 'making' the breakfast?

Me: Yes, I am 'making' the breakfast, I just asked you to get the coriander out the bag while I chop the onion, please? Why are you saying 'making' like that?

Mum: Well, you should 'make' the coriander come out the bag, then shouldn't you?

Me: Well, why can't you 'make' coriander come out the bag please?

Mum: I can, but that would mean I am 'making' the breakfast then wouldn't it?

Me: Erm, no, it just means you have assisted me in getting the coriander out the bag?

Mum: 'Assisted' yes, son, of course 😊

Me: Yeah, what else would it be?

Mum: I know what you're doing, remember I'm your mum.

Me: I just asked if you could get the coriander, that is it. What are you going on about, Mum?

Mum: You are trying to get Mum's touch on the food to ensure it tastes nice. Us mums, we know these things... don't worry, be confident... and make sure you fill my cup of tea to the top, sonny...

307

Corona Conversations:

Me: I feel you're coming too close to me,
Dad. We need to maintain social distance,
remember?

Dad: Don't worry, the state you live in, boy,
even Corona wouldn't come near you...

Mum: How many cups have you been using?

Me: Possibly three?

Mum: Why are you using three when you only have one mouth?

Me: Well I wanted to use seven — a different one for every day of the week…

Mum: Told you so many times, boy, don't try and be smart as it doesn't suit you... Use one and if you want another tea, wash the cup and use it again.

Me: Well, why do you have so many plates?

Mum: What did I just say to you about acting smart? You are not even making sense; the plates are for when guests come... so now what?

Me: I was just sayin'...

Mum: Less saying more doing, son... you do the washing up, and you do as I say then there will be no issue...

(Now talking to herself and/or Allah) My son can't even get one wife but needs three cups... Allah help him!

Cuppa, anyone...?

Deeper Introspections 4

Out of the billions of people in the world, why is it we meet the people we do? Islamic hadeeth suggests that the connections we make with others are predestined through a connection of our very souls that have known one another in a prior existence. A beautiful explanation indeed. What is for sure is that every person we meet, every person we connect to, is an opportunity to touch another's heart, to help them grow and through our interaction grow as human beings ourselves. In attempting to understand you, I understand a little more about me.

Notes

Perhaps it may be true to say each one of us has insecurities, just that maybe some hide it more than others — some of us even hide them away from our own selves, to the point where, ironically, we appear as confident and even arrogant in some instances. Deep down, maybe we all have self-doubt about our abilities and purpose and maybe if we each remember our essential human traits are essentially the same as those of every single other person, then maybe we can each give one another the chance to be ourselves and really shine...

Notes

Perhaps one of the most beautiful possibilities of our individual existence is that within each of us are the answers to one another's prayers.

Notes

All praise is to He, who hears even the very
quietest of words unspoken, never once touched
by even our own lips, yet tell the very story
of the essence of our silent soul...

Notes

We live in a world where our devices of connection increasingly cause us to disconnect, where often a woman's oppression is based on her choice of clothing and her liberation by the lack thereof, where we consume ever-increasing amounts, to the point we have nowhere to discard our waste, while others waste away from the lack of having anything to eat, where we send soldiers across continents to take control of commodities and nations and cultures are destroyed yet we speak of terrorism and 'national security'. Where man-made diseases are licensed by our governments, and billionaire tax evaders request the masses to charitably donate. Where we speak of the first and third worlds as if we are from different planets...

Notes

And maybe the very darkest moments of your life, are simply permitted to happen to enable you to recognise the power of your own light...

Notes

Your troubles are my troubles, your peace is
my peace, as a piece of you is a piece of me...

Notes

One can never be emotionally free, whilst psychologically imprisoned.

Notes

Social Commentary 4

Mental health issues, unlike us, do not discriminate. They are not exclusive to gender or age or race, nor may they be attributed to one's culture or religion. While it is undeniable that many find a level of peace of mind in their submission to their faith, it is both disingenuous to our understanding and factually inaccurate to attribute an individual's mental health issues to a lack of understanding of belief or proximity to their creator. At their base level, issues around mental health centre around an irrational belief that one's individual problems are bigger than oneself, leading to feelings of isolation and alienation from one's interrelationships both with others and with oneself.

Many, many of us will, at times, suffer mental health issues in varying degrees and such is the complexity of the essence of our being, in many cases, we may not overtly even be aware of our own suffering let alone the sufferings others have to endure.

It is not weak nor strange, neither is it different or weird, to feel challenged by the workings of our minds. Indeed, perhaps in the instances where individuals are aware and can actually articulate their thoughts and feelings, these individuals are examples of the strongest amongst us, as their suffering enables the rest of us to learn about our own selves and the fragility of the essence of our being.

Notes

Each and every one of us, if honest, is full of a multitude of vulnerabilities and whilst none of us can account for what is truly beyond the visible and outwardly apparent, we know we are here, right now, living in the present moment. Live. Live for one another as this is really no more than living for oneself, for surely we can never really do too much for another to feel loved, comforted, secure in this momentary instant of life. Know that each and every one of us is valid and worthy; as just as you are no better than anyone, know surely you are no worse...

As conversations start to become more open about this previously taboo topic, it is worth noting that rather than being on the periphery of societies, it is estimated 450 million people around the world suffer from a mental health disorder of some type.

Notes

World Mental Wealth Way...

On the outside, I have no injury
No one can tell what's happening to me
The emptiness that I feel inside
The depths of the traumas that reside
On the outside, I'm as happy as can be
That's how it seems apparently
No one sees my emotions bleed
Mental repression incapacity
And so, I must speak my truth
It is important I tell you
Not just so you know how injured I am
More just so that I know I can
And as long as I talk, I know I'm not captive
To these thoughts and feelings that come in
  their masses
Overwhelm and engulf and capture my breath
Almost to the point where there's none of me
  left
But as long as I talk, I know I can express
As long as I talk, I can work out the mess
And with each word I talk, I gain clarity
Slowly understanding the best of me
So, while I may have put you in an awkward
  position
Thank you, to you for your decision to listen
To listen, to engage, to care and be there
To make me feel like I did not overbear
The best of gifts to one another on earth
Is surely to increase each other's
  self-worth...

Notes

The Cracks of Dawn...

My irrational rationality
Plays with my sanity
I can't see care
In fact, I don't even dare
Isolated by my madness
Only recognising my sadness
Self-imposed solitary confinement
Mentally maligned, as I sit in my silence
A million voices speaking to me
Confused anarchy internally
A darkness deeper than the darkest night
Sometimes I wonder, why even bother to fight?
But then I remember even with the darkest
  night
It is always followed by morning light
And that morning light always shines bright
And just maybe this is what my emotional
  cracks are for?
Maybe each of them serves as a door?
To allow the most beautiful light to enter
To reach to my soul and allow me to be better
Maybe it's ok for me to break down
So that I know I can turn it around?
I read somewhere for a star to be born
That a nebula of gas must first collapse
And maybe this process is my journey,
  perhaps
To allow me in myself to see my new dawn...

Notes

Empathetic Reality

Surrounded by people yet feeling alone
Afraid to speak out for being seen to moan
If only they knew the pain in my heart
If only they knew how it tears me apart
So many thoughts make me delirious and manic
Cause my breath to shorten and attack and panic
Thinking things are so much bigger than me
Can't tell no one because of the bigotry
A feeling so deep it can't just be called sad
A feeling so deep it's driving me mad
And so, I keep to myself, not to be a burden
At least no one will know how of myself, I'm
  uncertain
At least they will simply see me as detached
Never know how my own thoughts attack
Overall, I think it's better this way
As what if anyone knew my dismay?
But then what if I went and told someone?
And what if that person listened and didn't run?
And what if they listened and simply cared
  for me?
And what if that care made me feel free?
And what if once free I could just be?
And then I could see a rationality?
That nothing is ever bigger than me?
Then my thoughts, my love, our shared
  humanity?
And what if I then believed in my
  self-worth?
My personal value and my place on earth?
How amazing the power of care and empathy
Breaking down our prisons of psychology
Allowing you to reach out to me
Allowing us all to all live in a better
  reality...

Notes

Know Your Self

You see the thing about knowing your own
  mental health
Is to know, it's only really you that knows
  yourself
Sometimes as bright and brilliant to the
  outside you may seem
Merely a mask for the dark and destructive
  inner self-esteem
A society built upon outer appearance
Never really knowing about your own
  perseverance
That keeps you going when there's no belief
While nobody else knows what lies beneath
To the outside world, you are nothing but
  friendly
Whilst inside yourself you are your own
  worst enemy
A psychological prison that keeps you
  depressed
Brought on by all the thoughts you have kept
  repressed
You see the thing about knowing about your
  own mental health
It's knowing you deserve to be just yourself
To know, to accept, to live and to love
To embrace all of you and know you're enough
To be aware of your blessings from above.
To know imperfection is not wrong
To know you have the right to belong.
You see the thing about knowing about your
  own mental health
Is to know your inner wellbeing is your true
  wealth...

Notes

Delusions of Difference

You know I've never really fitted in
Never really known where to begin
To be normal and part of everyone else
Never really felt like I can be myself
The clarity I can never seem to find
And I'm not even saying people ain't kind
It's just at the best of times
Even I just about understand me
So how can anyone else really?
Maybe I've never fitted the norm
Probably ever since the day I was born
At times I wonder just how it would be
Just for a little while if I wasn't me
Just for the pressure to release
Just to find some inner peace
Then sometimes just as I'm about to give up
  the fight
I feel within me that glimmer of light
Knowing no matter how confused my reality is
I still have much to offer and so much to give
And no matter how many times I fall
I can find a way to stand tall
And it's not despite all of my confusion
And it's not despite my emotional intrusion
Rather, it is for just these very reasons
I know I am strong and can keep believing
If I can accept and embrace all that I am
Even love myself and be my own biggest fan
Then I will slowly but surely grow to
  understand
That I have the ability to stand strong
Knowing that for these very reasons, we all
  belong...

Notes

Indifferent Differences

The thing is depression knows no
   discrimination
Refuses to check if you're Black, Asian
or Caucasian
It doesn't care much for the denomination
   you are,
Doesn't look if you're established, or
   you're a rising star
Its brother anxiety is not much different
Often comes around when we refuse to listen
And pay the attention and give love as it is
   needed
Encouraged by a society that is oh so
   conceited
A mentality encouraged of thinking only of
   the self
No consideration for the notion of
   collective wealth
For the fact that personal peace cannot be
   achieved alone
That in all our years of existence, no one
   has achieved on their own
And so, the result of it all is a society of
   stress
Everyone consumed with trying to be 'the
   best'
Individual illusions of what form success
   may take
Superficial realities, unreal and fake
Ignoring decrees of universal equality
Multiple egos thinking 'It's all about me'
When we all accept and embrace that we need
   one another
On that, we will all truly start to recover

Notes

Understanding that by starting to humble yourself
Is the first step on the path to our collective wealth...

Notes

Marks of Mentality

And at first it was my scars that held me
  back,
For fear of them being noticed and then
  being attacked
In a world where everyone seems so clean
What would they think knowing where I had
  been?
What would they say seeing my marks?
Created in a place that was so very dark?
Judging me saying it wasn't right
Judging from a place of light
Where they hadn't suffered my battles
Wouldn't really get what left me rattled
What didn't allow me to sleep
Left me with myself and my thoughts so deep
At first it was my scars that held me back
Then I realised was merely perceptions and
  nowhere near fact
My marks that made me question
Were no hindrance, but a lesson
A sign, not that I was weak
Moreover, of the strength I seek
An indication I could survive
A testament that I am alive
No matter the battles I face
I am bigger and I will embrace
A reminder I am still here
Knowing I am bigger than my fear...

Notes

Don't Be Afraid

Don't be afraid to stand out from the crowd
Don't be afraid to stand loud and proud
Don't misunderstand, it's not about foolish
  pride
Just don't be afraid to know you have nothing
  to hide
Don't be afraid to let your light shine from
  inside
Don't be afraid to recognise your worth
Don't be afraid to know your right of birth
Don't be afraid to celebrate your dignity
Don't be afraid to set yourself free
Don't be afraid to ask for the blessings of
  your maker
For surely, He is
Al Mussawir — The Beauty Shaper
Al Wahhab — The Giver
Al Razzaq — The Sustainer
Al Mugni — The Enricher
Don't be afraid to live with pure love on
  earth
Don't. Be. Afraid
Search and question for surely it is not
  only your individual right
But your obligation to question what you
  perceive to be lies
Search until not only your heart, but your
  intellect is satisfied
That you can search no more and that you are
  correct in your conclusion
That what you know is reasoned and without
  illusion
For surely all answers lead to one —

Notes

That of your own existence, our universal
  community and what He began
Al Baree — The Originator
Al Kaleeq — The Creator
Al Ghafoor — The Forgiver
Al Atheem — The Supreme
Al Raafi — The Elevator
Al Hafeedh — The Protector
Al Haaq — The Source of all Truth
And if your need is to search for more
As you knock on your very truth's door
Know that He is Al Wadood — The Source of all
  Love
For whom nothing is ever too much
Who will answer all in the best of ways?
As we journey through our nights and days...

Notes

Al Wali told me...

Come to success
You told me
Yet, I chased it everywhere else
Come to success
You told me
An opportunity to be myself
To express to You all my thoughts
The deepest of my heart
To be at peace with my soul
And address that which tore me apart
From the very essence, of who I was
And left me feeling lost...
Yet, for so long I didn't hear
Your calling to come near
Never really understanding
That You held me dear
I sought comfort in things of fleetingness
Inevitably for those things to pass
Mourning why those things had left me
Never realising they weren't meant to last
For You told me we're simply travellers
On a journey to a different place
To not lose hope and be sad — simply not to
   lose our faith
To always remember your presence
Was the essence of what You said
As you love each and every one of us
Even more than we can comprehend
I'm sorry for my betrayals and the doubts I
   had in You
For You are the only answer worthy of praise
   and true

Notes

I love you, never doubt me and always chose
  to forgive
Allowing that I am simply me and blessing me
  to live...

Notes

Deeper Introspection and
Social Commentary 5

Khadija Vs Culture

The First Lady of Islam who believed when no one believed, who provided reassurance whilst others mocked and belied, who provided comfort through her personage and financial wealth. The first person in the history of the world to bear witness and declare faith.

The dynamism of her astute business nature, resulting in her leading business status in a trading environment traditionally dominated by men, whilst all the while she married and divorced three times, with three different men and bearing children with all three.

Who then chose to ask the prophet PBUH for his hand in marriage who was a younger man over 20 years her junior in age.

This is the original love story of Islam.

The status and honour of woman symbolised through the choice of the Creator in Khadija RA. The best of examples... and yet our modern liberal collective cultures, both in our communities and societies without exception, betray the Creator's example. Our personal prejudices, cultured and shaped through our communities, do not only refuse to accept the honour of our Khadijas, more often they neglect and reject our women. Our toxic notions of what we may accept as 'correct' for the status of our women leading to a state of suppressed surviving for our sisters and

Notes

missed opportunities of collective growth and learning for us all.

The toxic infiltration of 'man-made' notions of masculinity to modern-day communities and cultures lead to a misogyny that is a betrayal to the very essence of the beginning of Islam and the symbolism of Khadija RA and the point of the Creator in His choice.

Let us give recognition, embrace, elevate, acknowledge our women for surely they are the very reason for our birth, physically, mentally and spiritually and celebrate them today and every day, for surely according to the Creator this is what is meant to be?

Notes

Behind the Burka

You tell me I'm oppressed
Because of the material that I wear
While you vilify and mock me
Causing at best an unwelcome stare
At worst, I am attacked
And told I don't belong
All the while you claim
You have said nothing wrong
And to you, I'm just another
Political point opportunity
To others, I am a woman
Mother of humanity
You claim I have no choice
Because of what men have forced upon me
All the while your political agenda
  reinforces misogyny
And for generations across borders
I have fought for my right to a choice
Yet here we are in this liberal land
Where you take away my voice
Tomorrow another issue
Of the latest controversy
And whether I choose to cover
Or let my hair run free
Know that I will live
Exactly as I want to be
Because far from your degradation
Is my right to liberty?
I will live by the freedom
Of my Lord's loving decree...

Notes

Wonder Woman

The real wonder of a woman is in the fact she stands against oppression and battles for her independence and rights, regardless of the systems that deny her.

The real wonder of a woman is in the fact she provides comfort and reassurance to make human-kind stronger.

The real wonder of a woman is her love for her family, love to her partner, guidance to her children and honour to her parents.

The real wonder of a woman is her recognition of others through her sisterhood and support.

The real wonder of a woman is that every woman is, in fact, the core of all humanity, in every society and community.

Around the world without exception, regard-less of race or religion. There are many women of wonder to be found everywhere in everyday lives, battling systems and cultures of patriarchy and misogyny and the sexism that is prevalent and the downfall of mankind.

Look around, everywhere the wonder of a woman is impossible not to see...

There ain't no real wonder woman on your film screens, clothed in fancy-dress by Hollywood men perpetuating cycles of misogynistic mentality.

Let's come correct if we are coming at all...

Notes

Social Commentary 6

We Belong

Mali to Burma
Christchurch to Gaza
Yemeni, Libya
Iraqi and Syria
Destruction of Arabia
No fine China
Implosion of India
People of Kashmir
Year on year
Living in fear
Mr. Islamophobia
Suppress and control
Calculating murder
Global Intifada
People rise up
Against the corrupt
Mr. Instigator
Original hater
Killer of freedom
Perceive us with derision
Supremacy mentality
Everybody's tragedy
Enemy funder
Pillage and plunder
Who makes hate?
News you make
Oppression unspoken
People left broken
Funded by the same
Leaders insane
Just because I'm black
You constantly attack
My Muslim faith
Never leaves me safe

Notes

Holding monopoly
Mentality of misogyny
Ethnic minority
Ethical majority
Walls you build
Your heart is sealed
Mr. Coloniser
Being better is whiter?
Steal and rape
Doesn't make you great
History of lies
Forgotten cries
Dismiss our belief
Our principle of peace
Yet for all you do
We hold true
Knowledge we seek
We are not the weak
We know we are strong
We know we belong
Crusades of crucifixion
To destroy my religion
Violence your tradition
Yet. Still
We belong
Regardless of politician
Who devises the division
While looking upon us with derision
We will belong
Adopted counting system
Just one example given
Your stolen knowledge mission
Thereafter history rewritten
To claim you gave us civilisation
Here we are
And rather than be hateful

Notes

Of subjugation upon us disgraceful
We're supposedly meant to be grateful
That We Belong
Maybe if the truth were represented
It would be you that resented
The lies you were presented
Created and indoctrinated
We belong
Here we are
To this very day
You continue to invade
To this very day
You continue to enslave
To this very day
Cause everyday tragedy
To this very day
Separating kids from their family
Liberal freedom fantasy
Democratic disparity
To this very day
Yet you are supposedly the civilised
Who is deaf to babies that cry
Who cares not for how many die
As long as you are the one in control
Care not that devil is the owner of your soul
Here we are
We won't sit in silence
We won't ignore the violence
The oppression
The suppression
As long as the world to the truth needs to be
  made wise
In the words of sister Angelou 'we will
  rise'
Because
We all belong

Notes

Pickup Your Belonging

The helpful and the helpless
The selfish and the selfless
The weak and the strong
To which group do you belong?
Those that give and those that take
Those that are real and those that are fake
To which group do you belong?
Those that need and those that receive
Those that reject and those that believe
Those that give out and those that give in
The ones that lose and the ones that win
Those that need to speak and those that need
  to listen
To focus on what is common or on what is
  different
The good and the bad
Those that make you happy and those that
  make you sad
To which group do you belong?
Are we all, without exception
Deception or misperception, part of both?
To recognise personal limitation is part of
  collective growth
To embrace individual inspiration, giving
  consideration Essential to integration and
What makes us all whole

Notes

& What If

& what if tomorrow I was not to awake
What would be my actual legacy?
Given the chance
What would I really think, looking back,
  just simply at me?
Would I have really done enough?
Given to the world and shown enough love?
Or would I be full of regret?
A life wasted one I choose to forget
Did I really make the most of every
  opportunity?
Valued everything that was presented to me?
& what if tomorrow I was not to awake?
Would I regret the chances that I didn't
  take?
For the fear of failure and the judgement of
  others
Pride destroying friendships and potential
  lovers
Relations ships that have long sailed away
Feeding my own Nafs a high price to pay
What if really, I wasn't to awake?
As one day that will really be the case
Could I really answer for all my actions?
Could I really say I honoured the intimacy
  of my interactions?
Could I honestly look back with dignity over
  my pride?
& really be of those with nothing to hide?
Truth is I'm full of hypocrisy
A constant battle just tryna be me
Apparently, it's all just a test
At school I cheated in those, I must confess

Notes

Maybe inside all of us, there's a bit of a
  mess
Maybe I'm not so different from the rest
of everyone else who seems to be 'living
  their best life'
Maybe, in reality, the hypocrisy is rife
One day, truth is, none of us will awake
So maybe we should all ask
'What we doing to make this world great?'
& rather than thinking about what we can
  take
Maybe it's really about what we each can
  give
To ourselves and to one another, so that we
  can all have a chance to live...

Notes

The Guest of Honour

Perhaps it is true to say
That we each to one another are
A guest of honour...
A special visitor
Whose presence should be cherished
And welcomed in the warmest of ways...
Perhaps we each are a guest of honour
To be offered the best we have to give
In the most timely of fashions
So, we do not even have to ask for
  consideration
As it is already given
In a way that will delight and amaze
Perhaps we are to one another
The best of gifts
Whose presence uplifts
And brightens the darkest of days
So, let us honour our rights
Each to each other
To enable us all to be
The most beautiful of lights
Guiding and giving
And in turn receiving
The most beautiful love
Graced from above...

Notes

Deeper Introspection 6

In our cities of millions, there are a million stories of struggles… Each of us living within our own existence, trying to make sense of a senseless world. The spirit of life is apparent in the eyes of our elders, a hint of a beautiful life lived and the energy of a soul that lives with wisdom beyond the restriction of their physical body, whilst the young feel eternity is theirs, and the rest of us live somewhere in between. Reach out. Reach out as far as we can physically, emotionally, spiritually. Reach with the very tips of your fingers to the very soul of your heart. Truly therein, whilst we may not find the answers we seek, we will find the answers we need...

Notes

Personal struggles and battles are relative to one's experiences and life and not to be compared to each other, as this is both unfair to oneself and nonsensical. Whilst we can each, with sincerity, offer perspectives on the conditions of one another, it is belittling and arrogant to assume to understand exactly what a person is feeling in their times of trouble. We can, however, be reassured of this unity; regardless of our individual experience, each and every one of us is a product of pure love and of the highest value, by the decree of living life itself and through whom it has been ordained. In moments of darkness, essentially this is the only reminder we need to give to ourselves, every part of us a miracle, even every drop of any tear we shed has the most precious of value, thus compelling us to shed them for only that which is truly worthy of the inner workings of one's heart...

Notes

It is easy for any of us to simply accept our current circumstances and situation as 'the norm'. Routines of actions and interactions very quickly seem as if they have always been so and indeed, often that they will always be so. Yet, all too often, in an instant, that which we knew as constant changes completely, invariably before any real chance to reflect, until moments are simply more than a set of memories. At one point in all our lives, we came home from a place we would never visit again, saw a beautiful friend without realising we would never see them again at the time and even in our situations of knowing, have had to let go of that which we hold most dear... Embrace each and every experience of life we are blessed with, that has brought us each to the point of now. Cherish the moments of light so that they may be our strength when we feel weak in our moments of darkness. In a life we each live where everything evolves and changes, let us allow our own love to be constant in order that it may become the very foundation that guides our paths, so we may walk the most beautiful of paths together...

Notes

The concept of 'Rizq' or 'the provision of what is due' is a source of both contentment and encouragement. From a personal perspective, it allows the opportunity to view the success of others with happiness as it does not allow the opportunity for envy and, further, it negates the futile practice of comparative success human beings often degenerate into. It provides the assurance that through one's own work and striving, what is meant to be in all eventuality will be, even if the outcome isn't what one has initially aimed and pursued. Above all, as with many of the dimensions of Islam, in a world and life of struggle and difficulty, it is yet another path to inner peace...

Notes

How strange the condition of humankind, wherein we continue to worship ourselves, insisting we are most high, whilst we deceive one another and commodify notions of emotions, relationships and love... Indeed, how strange the condition of humankind, wherein we reject our Creator, who compels us to nothing, other than that for His sake, we love and care for one another each and every single day...

Notes

And maybe our times of solitude and being alone are a reminder that not only are we sufficient, but that we are more than this, more than simply just 'enough'. For no matter how small and even awkward we may perceive our personal piece of the world to be, without each of us, the puzzle of our collective lives could never be complete.

Notes

And perhaps accepting the condition of our own human fragility is so intrinsic to our own unique being, that embracing those very sensitivities are essential to the very strengths we each need to grow...

Notes

If you define other people by their differences to yourself, be it colour, race, religion, gender or anything else, then you are not only part of the problem, you are the problem. The solutions to the problematic issues in our world are in the recognition of the oneness of our existence and reality. One humanity living within this one world. Through the acknowledgement of our unity, we find our individual security. Through the recognition of our equality, we each will live in a way that surpasses the barriers of oppression which suppress our psychologies. Through the understanding of our humility, we overcome the arrogance that deems us better than the 'other', and we live as one humanity. The out-ward path to peace begins with our internal steps of love towards it...

Notes

Love. With all of yourself, in each and every moment and do not ever be afraid of heartbreak, as it is through breaking, the essence of the soul opens, to live to become more than what it ever knew before…

Notes

And in our moments of muted silence, when even
the most articulate amongst us have nothing
to say, lost in the inaccuracy of our limi-
tations, His love is our constant light, a
beacon of guidance in this storm of life...

Notes

One of the most beautiful linguistic nuances of Islam may be how the believer is ordained to increase the greeting of peace on whomsoever greets them in peace. Thus 'peace' is met with 'peace and blessings' and so forth in accordance with the decree of the Creator. Literally, to be compelled to compete to grant blessings of peace and love upon one another from the very first instance of interaction and conversations...

Notes

Certainly, very few circumstances are simplistic in their nature just as we as people are multifaceted with many shades to our personalities. Often, knowing how to act or to act in 'the right way' isn't always clear and is obscure in interpretation. More often, if we are really honest, we create distortions ourselves to suit our perspectives of what we deem to be right. So, it may be argued to act from a position of love is the only choice we have. Real love will never allow our own dishonour and indeed for us to dishonour one another. While it makes us vulnerable, it is also our ultimate protection, ensuring the value we place on ourselves, through our treatment of others, is recognised with the value we all deserve.

Notes

'Speak Truth'. Seemingly a straightforward ideal which each of us lives by. A trait we encourage as we educate our young and a characteristic by which we measure the honesty of one's character as adults. And yet, such is the state of the world, more often than not, such is the rarity of the notion of truth, those that simply speak it are described as daring and heroic as if what they have done is the boldest and most difficult of tasks. Perhaps in our treatment of such individuals, in fact exists a truth in itself... Such is the state of our deluded existence within the illusionary societies where we exist and live, the recognition, enactment and speaking of truth is the most revolutionary of acts. In a world of emotionally psychological oppression, only truth itself enlightens our path to freedom.

Notes

The truth is you may not always get back what you give out. Your love, consideration, care and all those other 'positive' attributes may in fact actually never be reciprocated or even recognised and acknowledged in the instant that you present them. That's the truth... and what is also the truth is that that is OK, for in the essence of your soul, giving it has recognised the value of existing in the most honourable and beautiful of ways. In that very instant, whether anyone respects and rightly embraces this or not, you have given in the most blessed of ways, and you have truly understood what it means to really live.

Notes

'Where did the time go?'... A universal reminder to cherish the moments we each live as indeed time is constantly moving forward, waiting for no one. While planned breakaways and departures from people we knew and places we habituated are often sad, perhaps what is more profound is that in many of the instances and moments of life, our experience becomes 'the very last time' without even realising; the very last time as a kid meeting with our friends over the summer holiday that seemed to last forever, often simply to do the same nothing together every day; the last time as adults seeing people who were so part of our everyday existence we subconsciously assumed they would be there forever, as part of our normality and in a moment unplanned and unthought of, change occurs for us all. Retrospect invariably facilitates a nostalgic fondness over days gone by, especially in instances where our contemporary lives challenge our notions of being. Yet change, it would appear, is natural and universal, without prejudice or discrimination, something that happens to us all. Let us all live our lives encompassing this moment, whilst we learn and build from the foundations of our past, let us embrace each moment we live every day and today, for surely, without exception for all of us, these moments right here and now are our times...

Notes

Educate

Education is not simply a reflection of our academic attainment in accordance with the systems that are implemented through our schools, our colleges and universities. Moreover, to equate it as such is hugely restrictive and inaccurate, perpetuating the arrogance and division within societies, between groups of people who have accessed such systems and indeed are part of its very construction. The education of humanity resides within our understanding of our own humility, our equality as people and the realisation of the temporary nature of our existence.

Our thoughts and perceptions and our expression of them, through the way in which we articulate ourselves, are not just a reflection of our education; indeed they are the very nature of what it means to be educated, and as such, they are far beyond the attainments achieved within such systems simply implemented through institutions of curriculum agendas.
The violation of peoples is not simply reflected in wars with weapons of destruction. Indeed, violation starts in such systems, wherein actions and words of the derogatory abuse of groups of people are implemented through the disguises of intellectual debate, through words as weapons of mass distraction.

Our education is not to accept such violations, to object to and reject such systems of acceptance and those that seek to present them as acceptable.

Notes

Our education is to seek justice and celebrate our differences and our very right to live in a way that is fair. To understand that respecting others as we would ourselves is not only the most equitable choice we have, but the most beautiful of choices we could make.

Notes

The Islamic concept of Adhab may perhaps be best translated as good manners, social etiquette, courtesy and respect in the context of appropriate behaviours both public and personal. The notion of Adhab, amongst the most beautiful of nuances of behaviour from the Muslim world, often seems sadly forgotten.

Acknowledge and encourage, support and lift up each and every one that you are able to — everybody is indeed a somebody until the very moment we ignore them and deem them a nobody, seemingly because they are not important enough to acknowledge or we deem them not worthy enough of the limited time we all are restricted by.

Let us strive to embrace the very best of Adhab to ourselves and all human beings in each moment of life that we are blessed with — an active awareness that we invoke today will only serve to create a better and more beautiful tomorrow for us all... Insha'Allah

Notes

And So ...

I wouldn't say I'm a poet
Or at that, even a writer
I know multiples of people certainly more
   well-read and for sure, so much brighter
The point of my writing is to express
To make you think more and reflect
To acknowledge we all have a voice
Not to be suppressed but rather, rejoiced
For in the fact we can stand up and shout
About those things we feel so strongly about
Is the fact of the very essence of life
   itself
And surely a path to our personal wealth
So, my words are simply to serve the purpose
To show that we are each beyond those things
   that make us nervous
We are each a shining light as bright as can
   be
Each born of a product of the purest love,
   our existence evident miraculously
Let us grow collectively into new times
So that we each, all together, will be more
   than just fine
Let us embrace every moment there is to live
Recognising the miracle of the opportunity
   to give
To ourselves and to one another so that we
   each may find
A way to live our best lives leaving the bad
   behind
And even when, if bad occurs, we don't judge
   simply, be kind
Let us grow collectively into new times

Notes

Let me be strong for you so your strength can
  be mine
Opportunities to live like never before
More than you could think or ever saw
Blessings of love, honour and prosperity
Collectively understanding, embracing
  unity...

Notes

In every moment of every day, there are people everywhere, whose intention is to contribute towards positive change. Whether that be through their supplications and prayers to the Creator, researching new fields of academia and advancement in knowledge and understanding, being there for another simply in presence of mind, working beyond paid hours, learning new ways to live, caring about injustice and sharing their goodwill and concern, demonstrating, advocating, activating awareness and reacting to injustices. Simply, loving for the sake of love into the depths of deepest humanity in order to be the best of what it means to be humane. Such people are not the minority or rare in numbers, in fact, there are so many in numbers across all cultures and other apparent nuances of difference between us, we would simply never be able to identify them all, even within the space of a thousand lifetimes.

Whilst there is much to despair of in the world, and the narrative is often one saddening heartbreak, perhaps for this very reason, we would do well to remember and rejoice every so often that intrinsic to the essence of our being is to live every day in the best of ways, for each and everyone one of us is part of one family — human 'kind'... Subhana'Allah.

Notes

If you care, cry & feel guilt at the pain & suffering of others to whom you would seemingly have no direct connection or relationship too, be thankful. Be thankful for your tears. Be thankful for the sensitivity of your heart in that it longs to reach out to an empathetic reality, in amongst a world that wants you to be apathetic, desensitised & uncaring. Know, in that very moment your very soul has protested against both injustice & inequality and has reached out, transcending that which is beyond articulation on the most humanistic level.

Often, when we don't know what we should be saying or how we should be acting & searching for 'the right thing to do', it would serve us well to remember to question 'right by who?'

For some shouting in the streets is their protest, while for others silent prayers for peace are theirs, some may sign petitions, others may revise & review their own personal interactions. Protest takes many forms just as people themselves take many varied & wonderful forms. Everyone each has their own voice & as long as we persist in finding our own & resist the oppressive structures that want us to remain silent and simply not care at all, then through our struggles we are already becoming collectively more successful.

More Power to the People.

Notes

Our most sacred place of worship isn't in a distant land that requires permits & legal documenting and state permissions. The location of the greatest connection to our Creator is not to be found in any outward grand or magnificent building, built by the hands of humankind, regardless of its capacity to hold multiples of worshippers and its connections to ancient stories of the scriptures.

The most holy of places, that permits the most intimate of connections to The Creator of the world, resides deep within each and every one of us...Indeed with the rhythm of our heart beat, is the music of our soul and if we listen to ourselves with His grace & permission, we may align ourselves to the most beautiful of blessed connections...

Notes

Across the world and throughout history, people of varying denominations of religious beliefs and different races have loved one another, simply for the sake of love. The psychology of divisions and hate set upon us serve nothing more than suppressive rule and control set by those entities that stand against collective humanity and unity. Indeed, perhaps it is true to say that love does not endure despite our perceived differences as individuals, but moreover, love exists because of a clarity within our perceptions and our deeper understanding of them. Love is our humanity, love is our equality, bringing us together as one human family. Our collective history teaches us that in the beginning and the end, real love will always overcome, spreading its brightest of lights even into the darkest of hearts.

Notes

Parental Poetry 2

Me: I have enough new material for my fifth book now.

Dad: You talk so much rubbish, you got enough material for 50 books, son.

Me: Thank you maybe I will write 50.

Mum: So, where are all these books then? How comes we've never seen them?

Me: Well, at the moment they are e-books, so you have to get them online on Amazon.

Mum: Well, what if you don't like going to Amazon?

Dad: He's appealing to the other Junglee's like him; they all like the Amazon.

Notes

The End.